LESSONS FOR NONPROFIT AND START-UP LEADERS

LESSONS FOR NONPROFIT AND START-UP LEADERS

Tales from a Reluctant CEO

Maxine Harris and Michael B. O'Leary

ROWMAN & LITTLEFIELD
Lanham • Boulder • New York • London

Published by Rowman & Littlefield
A wholly owned subsidary of The Rowman & Littlefield Publishing Group,
Inc.
4501 Forbes Boulevard, Suite 200, Lanham, Maryland 20706
www.rowman.com

6 Tinworth Street, London, SE11 5AL, UK

British Library Cataloguing in Publication Information Available

Library of Congress Cataloging-in-Publication Data Available

ISBN: 978-1-4422-7653-6 (cloth : alk. paper)
ISBN: 978-1-4422-7654-3 (electronic)
ISBN: 978-1-5381-3941-7 (paper : alk. paper)

♾ ™ The paper used in this publication meets the minimum requirements of
American National Standard for Information Sciences Permanence of Paper
for Printed Library Materials, ANSI/NISO Z39.48-1992.

For Helen

CONTENTS

INTRODUCTION

Every year thousands of nonprofit organizations, start-up companies, and small businesses open their doors. Some are motivated by a big vision, some by an altruistic mission; others have an innovative product or a novel process for making things work better. But what almost all of them have in common is that their founders know very little about business or what helps new ventures succeed or, as in most cases, fail. Despite coming from diverse worlds, they almost all confront the same issues of organizational culture, power and authority, hiring, problem solving, and dealing with the world outside their doors. They have to be aware of how they are seen, how their ideas grow into products or services, and how they will sustain themselves over time.

Consider this book the advice of someone who's been there (sometimes reluctantly). It's intended for all those driven, focused founders who have to confront the struggles of starting, running, and sustaining a business.

We begin with the story of one particular start-up behavioral health organization, Community Connections, which opened in 1984 in Washington, D.C. Within fifteen years, Community Connections grew to become the largest nonprofit behavioral health care organization in the nation's capital. Within thirty years, it was serving three thousand men, women, and children and employing four hundred people. It currently has an annual budget of $35 million and owns a real estate portfolio in excess of $46 million.

Just how did that happen? How did the *mission and vision* to provide high-quality behavioral health care and safe community living for
people whose mental illnesses had caused them to become disenfranchised from the rest of society turn into the *organization* called Community Connections?

In the early 1980s, while the founders of Community Connections
were building their organization, faculty at places like Georgetown University were teaching, doing research, studying successful businesses,
and writing papers. These two worlds existed in relatively parallel uni-
verses back then. Now, in this book, we try to bring together the experience and insights from the leader of an in-the-trenches behavioral
health organization and a former nonprofit consultant turned business-
school scholar/teacher.

Many books on management use a case study approach as a vehicle
for illustrating how organizations grow and thrive. Often the cases involve large, well-known organizations, and it can be hard to apply the
lessons learned to smaller companies in the early stages of their development. Sometimes books focus on one company exclusively. At other
times, shorter vignettes are combined from several organizations. While
this latter strategy may illustrate the universality of certain issues, it can
be hard for readers new to the business world. After a while, a short
vignette from one company seems to blend with other examples, and
those unfamiliar with the business world may find themselves getting
lost.

Other books, like *Five Temptations of a CEO* by best-selling author
Patrick Lencioni, invent a fictional business, describe how it deals with
a range of problems, and then provide commentary on the decisions
made by the imaginary company.[1] As engaging as this style can be, it
runs the risk of confusing the reader who is disinclined to trust a hypo-
thetical case where all of the variables are controlled by the author to
make a point. For some, it may lack a certain authenticity.

Not everyone learns in the same way. Some of us like factual information. We want to know what we can learn from the business or
academic world, a world in which research and data form the basis of
knowledge. For others, information comes from actual case studies of
how similar organizations coped with their challenges. "Oh, tell me
what happened. How did you deal with that problem?" A book that uses
case studies invites the reader to have a "conversation" with someone

who has had similar experiences. "How can I learn from what you did right and what you did wrong?" *Lessons for Nonprofit and Start-Up Leaders: Tales from a Reluctant CEO* uses a real organization, Community Connections, to bring to life the actual conflicts that an organization (particularly a founder-run midsized business) must confront and solve if it is to survive and be successful. The book takes the reader through the challenges of building and sustaining an organization: whom to hire; how to solve problems; how and when to engage the community and other external stakeholders. We have written this book in an attempt to help readers understand that they can do it too—and perhaps avoid some mistakes along the way by seeing how it unfolded at Community Connections.

Some people learn best when their imaginations are engaged. It is no surprise that every culture, from the Maori in New Zealand to the Navajo in North America to the Danish in Western Europe, has a tradition of fairy tales—stories of fanciful creatures and naive protagonists, set in an imaginary land, in a time long ago. As these stories engage our imaginations, they teach us a moral lesson, a way to solve a problem, or an explanation for how things work in the world. We read them, or more often listen to them, for amusement or pleasure. But when the story is over and we leave the world of fantasy, we look up and realize that we have learned something.

In *Lessons for Nonprofit and Start-Up Leaders*, we attempt to meld all three of these ways of knowing into a single coherent whole. The case studies come from Community Connections, an organization founded by Maxine Harris and Helen Bergman. Each case study illustrates a unique theme, with particulars drawn from several separate incidents. The names of the people involved are invented, and the story itself is a composite of similar events that occurred over a span of thirty years. Of course, it must be said that case stories are always a product of memory. No one example is recorded exactly as it happened. The fairy tales come from our collective imagination, or, as the storyteller might say, "They were plucked from the air." The academic commentary is provided by Michael O'Leary, a professor of leadership at Georgetown University's McDonough School of Business.

We asked ourselves, "What would happen if we started every chapter with a fairy tale, a myth involving naive characters set in a place outside of time, away from everyday existence?" The reader—especially the reader not usually inclined to pick up a management book but one struggling with management issues nonetheless—would become engaged in a story that indirectly introduced a business dilemma and laid out new ways to understand choices in running a company. We would follow with a case story from the work at Community Connections and conclude with a discussion and a perspective that would come from current research and more theoretical formulations. A little something for everyone.

What emerged was a structure addressing eight different issues that Community Connections wrestled with and that are encountered by almost every founder-run organization.

In chapter 1, "Every Organization Has a Culture of Its Own: The Beginnings of Community Connections," the authors discuss the circumstances surrounding the birth and growth of Community Connections and how experiences, pitfalls, struggles, and successes helped to shape the culture of the organization. The importance of the relationship between the two founders is also highlighted as an important factor in shaping the eventual direction that Community Connections took.

The fable of "Two Girls" reminds the reader that curiosity and fun are also part of starting a new business. It is not all struggles and mistakes. And it is often curiosity and grit that keep organizations going during tough times.

The authors conclude the chapter with a more formal discussion of just what constitutes culture and why culture matters. They discuss how culture comes into being and what it means for an organization to have a strong culture.

In chapter 2, "How to Make an Idea Come Alive: Inspiration, Thinking It Through, and Making It Happen," the focus shifts to how founders move from an idea or a vision to something that has real meat on the bones. All socially driven businesses and creative endeavors start with an idea, an inspiration that drives the decision to open up shop. But a bright idea is not enough. Thinking and implementing are at the core of the success of any start-up. The chapter uses examples from the history of Community Connections to show what happens when all three are aligned and what can go wrong when they are not.

The fable "A Tower to Reach the Sky" tells the story of a boy who sees a glorious shooting star and then finds others who help him build a tower to the heavens. His vision, spectacular as it is, is not enough to build the tower alone.

The chapter concludes with a discussion of design thinking as an approach to innovation and applies its core concepts to Community Connections and other similar organizations. Design thinking emphasizes both a deep emotional understanding on the part of the stakeholders in any business venture and the value of the collaborative generation of ideas.

Chapter 3, "Power, Authority, and Responsibility: Who's in Charge Around Here?" initiates a discussion of the all-important dimension of power within an organization. When mission-driven organizations begin, the last thing they think about is power. Usually there are only a few founders and great consensus on just how things are to be done. But as an organization grows, questions arise as to just who is in charge and who bears responsibility for the success of the organization.

"The Magic Ring" tells the story of two brothers who begin as joint owners of a magic ring that confers great power, but as the fable continues, the brothers struggle and only one remains in possession of the ring. The chapter concludes with a discussion of the social science of power and shared leadership.

Chapter 4, "Hiring: People to Help With the Work," tackles problems that arise as organizations grow and expand. It may only take a few people to start a business, but it takes many more to actually run it. So how do you go about hiring new staff? Do you design the job and then hire the best person, or do you find good people and then let them create their own jobs? These are not simple questions as organizations move into the more complicated stages of growth. These are also questions that begin to require a more in-depth knowledge of how organizations work.

"The Clothing in the Chest" is a fable that tells the story of a girl who distributes clothing she has found in an old chest to a group of villagers who are shivering in the cold winter. But her distribution is based more on her need to feel generous and less on an assessment of what will actually fit each villager well. It is not surprising that most of the villagers are left with ill-fitting clothing and they make a pledge to be less eager and more thoughtful the next time an opportunity presents itself.

The chapter concludes with a discussion of talent management, a process that moves beyond simple hiring to managing an employee's needs and skills over the course of a career.

In chapter 5, "Barriers to Solving Problems: There Must Be a Way Around This," the authors address a concern ubiquitous in all new businesses, and in business in general: how to understand and solve problems. Even when everyone agrees as to what the problem is and how it might be addressed, there are still systemic and relational issues that prevent a clean solution. It is not always the case that there is unanimous agreement as to just what constitutes a problem. Differing perspectives add another barrier and a further difficulty in solving problems, especially in new organizations where standard practices do not exist.

In the fable "Crossing the Woods," a girl decides to risk her safety and cross a dark forest. She faces a variety of challenges on her journey and needs to figure out how to evaluate and solve each problem and all of the barriers she must overcome along her way.

The chapter closes with a discussion of how the way in which a problem is framed has a decisive impact on the solutions that are attempted. The authors also consider the advantages and disadvantages of collaborative problem solving.

Organizations do not exist in isolation, so in chapter 6, "Engaging the Outside World: Is Anyone Out There?" the authors turn their attention to how organizations deal with the world outside of their own boundaries. At some point in its evolution, an organization needs to turn its attention outward, toward the community and the context in which it does business. Who are its potential partners? Where is the competition coming from? What changes in the external environment will have the greatest impact? For an organization that has survived and even thrived in isolation, this turning outward can bring struggles and conflict. In chapter 6, the authors present examples of what happens when there is too little engagement with the world outside the organization and what happens if there is too much. An example is provided that demonstrates the right amount of collaboration with the world outside the business.

The fable of "The Three Brothers" tells the story of three brothers and their very different ways of dealing with the world outside of their small homes. Each brother has a different strategy and those strategies result in very different outcomes. The chapter identifies four different strategies of interaction with the world outside the organization and suggests how these strategies might benefit or harm the organization.

In chapter 7, "The Importance of Self and Organizational Awareness: Taking a Hard Look," the authors turn back to the world inside the organization and consider what it means for an organization and its founders to undertake a serious self-assessment. Of course, self-assessment should be an ongoing part of running an organization. Continual reflection and adjustment to feedback is critical to success, but too much time spent looking at what you are doing, rather than doing it, can become navel gazing and lead to failure.

In "A Face in the Mirror," a young boy laments that he does not know what he looks like and would not be able to recognize himself. He embarks on a journey that takes him many places while he searches for his one true "face."

Making an accurate judgment about oneself is not just difficult in business. The chapter concludes with a discussion of the discrepancies in self-perception and perception made by others.

The final chapter before the conclusion is chapter 8, "Preparing for the Future: What's Next?" Questions of how to leave an organization that one has created and what needs to be done in order to ensure that an organization is sustained beyond the tenure of the founders are always difficult. Even in a relatively young organization, leaders need to have one eye to the future. What new development might be coming along and how can we prepare for it? Many businesses have a short life span because of a failure to plan ahead. This chapter addresses issues of scalability, sustainability, and succession.

The fable "Little One Note" addresses the concerns of a clan member who is always afraid of the future and the impact she has on the larger group.

In the chapter's conclusion, the authors pay special attention to issues of sustainability and succession. Both of these have to do with whether or not an organization will survive. Small businesses in particular have only a 50 percent chance of surviving and family-owned businesses rarely make it to the third generation of owners.

Although these eight chapters do not cover all of the issues that new businesses might face, they do present a wide enough range to give some guidance. We hope it increases the probability that readers' own organizations are successful—whether they are nonprofits, family businesses, or small corporations.

A PERSONAL NOTE FROM MAXINE

It always seemed right that the word "reluctant" should be part of the title of this book. But as we came to the end, I asked myself, "reluctant about what?" Surely, Helen, my partner and the cofounder of Community Connections, and I had never been reluctant about leaving a big public hospital that had already seen its best days, and we were not reluctant about being in charge. Helen ran a hospital ward where she made most of the decisions and I wanted to run my own shop shortly after I arrived at the hospital. So where was the reluctance coming from? Not from leaving the hospital, not from running our own program, but instead it came from the word "CEO." Just what did it mean to be a CEO? Having not come from a business background, we really didn't know, and we had only a vague sense that it was going to be something different from everything we had been trained to do. That's where the reluctance came from, not that we were about to leap into something new, but that we didn't know what that something was going to be.

I

EVERY ORGANIZATION HAS A CULTURE OF ITS OWN

The Beginnings of Community Connections

I remember an interaction with one of my first employers who told me that I should avoid putting anything personal in my office: no family photographs, no pictures on the wall, not even books on the shelves. His rationale was that I did not want to give away any information about who I was. I would thus have an advantage in every interview, every negotiation, and even every casual conversation I had.

But that employer could not have been more wrong. My empty office said as much about who I was as an office cluttered with papers and coffee cups would have. We can't hide who we are no matter how much we may try.

And just as people have identities, so do organizations. You can feel the culture of an organization the minute you walk in the door. The personnel, the space, the roles that people occupy, all say something about "who" this organization is. Culture is not static; it grows and changes over time in response to pressures from inside and outside the organization. The fable that follows captures the origins of a relation-ship (and a nascent organization), which are often visible only in retrospect.

A FABLE: TWO GIRLS

Once upon a time there were two little girls who loved to play in the grass. Each day they would run to the big field that adjoined their two homes and begin to play their favorite game. But one day the girl with the dark curls looked up and said to her friend with the long blond hair, "I am tired of this game. We know all the rules and we each play in just the same way. We need a new game."

"But a new game will be hard to find," said the girl with the long blond hair. "We may search and search and never find a game that we like as much."

"Don't be silly," said the girl with the curls. "Let's run down the hill and see what we can find."

The girls began running so fast that they stumbled and slid until they landed at the bottom of the hill with a thud.

"Now see what you have done," said the girl with the blond hair. "We have skinned our legs and ruined our pretty dresses."

"Yes," said her friend, "but I think we may have found a new game!" The two friends huddled together and began to write the rules for their new game.

Yet after a while the same thing happened: the girls grew bored with their game. This time it was the girl with the long blond hair who said, "I am tired of this game. It is no longer our special secret; everyone in the whole town knows how to play."

Once again the girls set off looking for a new game. This time they met a big bear who began to tell them of a game he played with his cubs (in those days bears could talk just like we do).

The girls listened and nodded their heads in unison, "Now this is a really good game. No one will ever know how we discovered this most remarkable game." The girls thanked the bear, gave him a big hug (something bears love), and set off to play their new game.

And so it went for many years, until one day one of the girls fell silent and began to weep. "Someday there will be no new games to play."

Then her friend turned to her with a big smile. "Now you are really being silly. There will always be new games." And so it was until this very day.

Good ideas, new ideas emerge from the lucky combination of the right people, a creative vision, an opportunity, and plenty of hard work. And, like the girls in the story discover, there is no shortage of new ideas. The girls in the story refer to their efforts as a "game" they love to play. Everyone who has founded a mission-driven business knows there is a sense of passion and creativity and fun at the start of a new project. Founders take on the challenge of doing something different and doing it differently. The girls in the story are in search of ever better innovations on the games they "love to play."

THE STORY OF COMMUNITY CONNECTIONS

In the early summer of 1977, the two founders of Community Connections met while working on a ward at St. Elizabeths Hospital, a three-thousand-bed public psychiatric hospital in the District of Columbia. Helen Bergman was a clinical social worker and Maxine Harris was a clinical psychologist. For both of them it was their first professional job after graduate school. Within seven years they opened what was to become the largest not-for-profit behavioral health care center in the District of Columbia. A place called Community Connections.

St. Elizabeths Hospital, founded in 1855 with the help of mental health pioneer Dorothea Dix, had once housed eight thousand patients who were cared for by four thousand staff. During its heyday, it was a center for research and cutting-edge care, but by the late 1970s when Harris and Bergman arrived to begin their careers, the hospital had fallen into disrepair. Much of the care was delivered by untrained paraprofessionals, the buildings were literally crumbling, and the patients wandered the grounds with blank stares on their faces. Diagnosed with depression, mania, and psychosis and medicated with powerful psychotropic drugs, some men and women were restrained in strait jackets, held down with physical restraints, and thrown into small windowless seclusion rooms in an effort to control their behaviors. The average length of stay for patients was seven years, and many individuals spent most of their adult lives being treated on sterile hospital wards and wandering the almost twenty-five acres known as the "campus."[1]

Wards were large and cavernous and housed up to fifty patients who sat listlessly on chairs that encircled the main room, patients who had little to no contact with one another or with the ward staff. Even staff passed one another without speaking and walked quickly through the tunnel that connected the two sides of the hospital grounds. Relational connection of any kind was absent.

And while some might argue that the hospital comprised a community of its own—complete with fire department, large kitchen garden, and chapel—it was completely cut off from the community outside its walls. The outside world was not only unknown, it was frightening, and in the words of one patient who had spent her life at St. Elizabeths, "They kill people like me out there."

St. Elizabeths felt more like a prison and less like a place where people could get care and become well. The mentally ill residents of the District of Columbia deserved better.

The story that unfolds in this chapter is the story of two women who rejected what they saw and created a new way of treating men and women with serious mental illness.

The Relationship

Before there was even an idea, there was a relationship between Maxine and Helen. In the summer of 1977, each not quite thirty years old, the two met at St. Elizabeths Hospital. Their first months at the hospital had been quite different. Bergman was working as a social work intern on a ward set up to train psychiatric residents. The patients were among the youngest treated at the hospital and considered not quite chronic. And there was an atmosphere of learning and hopefulness. Senior psychiatrists conducted clinical rounds and everyone knew that "B Building" (as it was called) was not a forever place, at least not for the staff.

In contrast, Harris, a newly minted PhD, was assigned to work on a chronic ward known as "M Building" with patients who babbled and screamed and chewed on cigarettes butts. Her immediate supervisor, who worked in another building, gave her little guidance and seemed more interested in talking about how Harris felt working at the hospital than about how she might help her patients. Not unlike the people on the wards, Harris felt lost and spent a good part of her first several months escaping to the hospital library, reading old psychiatric journals, and plotting how she might escape from St. Elizabeths.

These two divergent experiences were important because they formed the backdrop against which Community Connections was first conceived.

Despite this contrast in their first experiences at the hospital, when Harris and Bergman met they felt an almost immediate rapport. Coincidentally, they had been born three days apart in 1948; they were married one week apart in 1969; and they were both now in the process of getting divorced—a similarity that felt somewhat uncanny, reminding both of them of a song one of the psychotic women on the ward used to sing when she wandered the grounds, "We're twins! We're identical twins!"

Now not all new businesses start with such a similarity between the two partners, but this sense of "knowing" one another made it easier to work through some of the most difficult times in the life of Community Connections.

Over the next two years, Harris and Bergman had several conversations about both the theory and the practice of providing care for chronic, marginalized psychiatric patients. They also became each other's best friend, sharing a sense of mutual trust that, like the characters Thelma and Louise in the classic movie, allowed them to hold hands and drive off the cliff together when the right time came. But we are getting ahead of ourselves.

Bergman had now become a senior social worker, running a ward similar to the one on which she had trained, and Harris had transferred to the department that trained all hospital psychologists and supported a large program for training young psychologists from around the country. They began to formulate a plan for how to merge their two skill sets and develop a program that would allow them to experiment with a new way of treating patients.

From their separate vantage points, they began to observe that a large number of patients seemed to stay on the wards for months and even years without any noticeable change in their behavior. Patients complained about the conditions on the wards, but when given a chance to receive treatment in the community, they stayed out for only a short time until they became symptomatic and returned to the hospital. This "revolving door" looked as if it would go on forever.

At the same time, Harris observed young trainees being taught variants of the "talking cure," which, while interesting, seemed to have little impact on improving the condition of patients at St. Elizabeths. The hospital seemed attached to the patients and the patients seemed attached to the hospital. But these attachments seemed to have very little to do with actual treatment.

During this same period, the District of Columbia was in the midst of a class action suit (which lasted for thirty-seven years, from 1974 to 2011) filed on behalf of William Dixon and other patients that mandated community-based treatment options for patients hospitalized at St. Elizabeths. When the city failed in its efforts, the public mental health system was placed into receivership. One of the pro bono lawyers representing Dixon called the hospital "a crumbling, wretched institution . . . where in no sense of the word did the city treat the folks who were captured in the mental health system in a tolerable civilized fashion."[2]

As city officials became increasingly desperate to resolve the Dixon lawsuit, mental health administrators became more open to creative solutions. Harris and Bergman began to see that there might be an opportunity for real change.

The Idea

The broader mental health field was supporting a community-based intervention called case management. Patients would have their service needs managed by community-based clinicians who would connect them to resources ranging from housing to primary care.

Harris and Bergman had seen that patients needed more than resources, however. They needed relationships. And the connection that many of them felt with the hospital, however minimal it might be, would need to be replicated in the community if patients were to succeed outside of the hospital. Patients would need relational (or what came to be called clinical) case management.

But Harris and Bergman were not quite ready to launch their new model of clinical case management. They wanted more proof that it would work. With the support of the chief of psychology training, and the affirmation of clinicians with national reputations, they tested their model on one of St. Elizabeths wards. With Bergman's administrative skill and Harris's training credentials, they were able to staff the ward with young trainees and focus their efforts on working with patients who were involved in this cycle of the revolving door.

The new ward was built around the following core beliefs:

1. Those who have been marginalized and disenfranchised by virtue of psychiatric illness, violence and abuse, poverty, and race should be afforded high quality, state of the art behavioral health care.
2. People grow and thrive in connection to other people.
3. Integration into a "normal" community is not only a sign of respect; it promotes healthy living.

Each clinician was educated in how to access local resources and each was assigned a small group of patients whom they would get to know and with whom they would have a chance to form relationships. Clinicians would focus on the strengths and goals of each patient (now referred to as a client) and would help prepare clients for life in the community. The relationships forged in the hospital would be transferred to the community. Case management would become dynamic; it would become clinical.

COMMUNITY CONNECTIONS IS BORN

With an idea clearly articulated and tested, Harris and Bergman were now ready to put their program into practice outside of St. Elizabeths. Both could see that the trends in mental health were moving away from inpatient programs, even innovative ones. The Dixon court case would likely mean less money was going to be spent on the big public hospital.

With a small grant from the city government, initially won on the merits of its innovation but ultimately secured through relationships with city officials, the founders opened Community Connections in the summer of 1984. Located in a single townhouse, literally across the bridge from St. Elizabeths, Community Connections began with just three employees—Harris, Bergman, and Harris's mother—and a commitment to serve thirty-five patients who were to be released from the hospital. Now these were not the revolving door patients for whom Harris and Bergman had designed their model of clinical case management, but rather a group of long-stay patients who had resided at St. Elizabeths for several years. The city needed to outplace patients in order to comply with the Dixon mandate. Community Connections needed a contract . . . and so began a complicated alliance.

Within a period of twelve months, Harris and Bergman needed to find homes and supports for thirty-five men and women and make sure they did not return to institutional care. This meant working with land-lords, managing crises, even soothing a client in the middle of the night, all to make sure they did not go to an emergency room and thus back to the hospital. It also meant teaching people skills and helping them to find the resources to live in the community. The early culture was not only "can do" but it was "must do." The two worked long hours and did everything that needed to be done, including feeding clients a hot lunch (made by Harris's mother) to making sure they had a place to go for Christmas. As with many start-up organizations, Harris and Bergman worked many hours and often put Community Connections ahead of family and other obligations.

One year passed and the partners were successful: no rehospitaliza-tions, thirty-five people living in community homes, stories in the local paper showing Harris and Bergman moving a young man into his first home, carrying his clothing up the front stairs in two large plastic bags.

Now more and more contracts came their way. They no longer had to argue that clinical case management could work. They had proof to show that it did. With only one year of hard-won success, Harris thought it was time to go public. Clinical case management was not only a model for how to help clients in the District of Columbia move into the community, it was a whole new way of thinking about how to serve people with chronic mental illnesses. In1993, Harris and Bergman edit-ed a book on clinical case management.[3]

But again, let's not move too fast. It was one thing to find housing for thirty-five individuals, it was quite another to find community living for the second and third wave of clients, now totaling several hundred.

At first, Harris and Bergman contracted with a number of "mom and pop" homes where former patients lived together as a pseudo family. It soon became apparent that many of these homes were mini-institutions, with strict rules, meals served at five, patients in bed by eight, and no activity other than staring at the television. Clearly, Harris and Bergman could do better.

Just two years after they opened Community Connections, Harris and Bergman bought their first property designed to provide housing for their clients. A large building, with space for congregate living as well as four separate supported but independent apartments, was set up to provide housing for twelve clients. It was staffed around the clock and was focused not only on giving people housing, but also on teaching the skills clients would need to fully integrate into the community. Groups focusing on training were run by staff and trained interns, the first of whom stayed on and eventually ran the entire group living program at Community Connections. Clinical case management had moved into the world of residential services.

Over the next twenty-five years, Community Connections purchased forty-six properties and provided housing for more than five hundred people, most of whom now live in independent apartments subsidized by the District of Columbia and the federal government. Community Connections continues to provide clinical support to most of those residents.

But not everyone makes the transition from the hospital to the community smoothly. Some individuals became symptomatic, refused engagement with their clinical case managers, and lost their housing. It was not long after Community Connections opened its doors that the problem of institutionalization was followed by the problem of homelessness. In the late 1980s, Community Connections applied for and was awarded a grant to work with homeless women. Because of their vulnerability to violence and abuse on the streets, these women needed additional support services. In 1988, Harris interviewed the first twenty-five women referred for homelessness services. These interviews formed the basis of a book published in 1991 under the title *Sisters of the Shadow*.[4]

In order to fully integrate into their communities, individuals need more than just housing. They need meaningful activity and work. Once again, Harris and Bergman sought outside support to help them start an employment program. In the late 1980s the Dole Foundation funded a project to find employment for people with psychiatric disabilities. And while it was not until the mid-1990s that Community Connections partnered with research psychiatrists at Dartmouth Medical School to start an active supported-employment program, this first effort enabled Harris and Bergman and their growing staff of clinical case managers to understand just how much planning and effort it would take to help people who had spent their days sitting on wards to become working adults.

Clinical case management was now making its way into residential, employment, and homelessness services, but there was a lot more to come.

NEW IDEAS TO SOLVE NEW PROBLEMS OR ONE THING LEADS TO ANOTHER

Given that the goal of Community Connections and the clinical case management model was to help seriously mentally ill women and men find a place of dignity and self-worth in the community, it made sense that decent housing resources and job opportunities would be part of making that goal a reality. The founders of Community Connections were prepared for those challenges. What they were not prepared for were the other problems that arose when people with few coping skills, severe psychiatric symptoms, few practical resources, and fractured interpersonal relationships tried to live on their own—even with support from Community Connections clinicians—in a community that was often less than welcoming and sometimes downright hostile.

On some occasions, clients felt so unsafe in their new homes that they left them for the streets. At other times, clients could not manage the tasks of maintaining a home and were hassled by landlords or other tenants for leaving doors open, not taking out the trash, or allowing strangers to camp in the hallways.

When clients lived at the hospital, they had a place to stay; when they were first placed in a community residence, they had a home. But when they failed to manage the rigors of independent living, they had homelessness.

Community Connections worked to address the problem of homelessness with aggressive outreach, finding people in parks and alleyways, and by designing a range of living options—group homes, shared apartments, supported independent apartments, and single occupancy rooming houses. Community reintegration remained the goal; we just had to find housing that would meet the varying needs of clients.

The streets can be dangerous places and people with poor judgment are likely to make devastating mistakes. Shortly after Community Connections opened, the District of Columbia experienced an epidemic of crack cocaine use. Initially, crack was cheap. It was highly addictive and mixed poorly with psychiatric medications, so once people became addicted to crack, they stopped taking their prescribed medications. Smoking a crack pipe in the park was a way for isolated people to "make friends." Enter the problem of drug use and addiction.

Community Connections never intended to be a drug treatment program, in fact, in the District of Columbia, substance abuse treatment and mental health treatment were housed in and regulated by two different branches of the Department of Health. But we found ourselves having no choice. Either we learned how to treat our clients' addictions or we would be helpless in accomplishing our primary mission of reintegrating them into healthy communities.

In 1991, we applied for and were awarded a federal grant to design treatments specifically for people who suffered from both a major mental illness and an addictive disorder, a problem known as a dual diagnosis. This new program required hiring not only additional staff, but also staff with different skills. Community Connections partnered with academic researchers because the grant involved not just designing services, but measuring their effectiveness. What was once a small service organization was becoming a center for research and clinical innovation. By the mid-1990s, Community Connections served between 450 and 600 dually diagnosed adults (addiction and mental illness), staff wrote articles and gave presentations, both nationally and locally, and Community Connections became recognized as a leader in the treatment of dually diagnosed individuals. This reputation led to a privately funded five-year study of treatment for dually diagnosed individuals that involved researchers from three major universities. It was at this time that Community Connections inaugurated a department of dual diagnosis services.

Addiction is not a stand-alone problem. Addicts get involved with the criminal justice system and women often prostitute for drug money and expose themselves to HIV infection. Dually diagnosed men and women are exposed to trauma and abuse, and families where parents struggle with addiction breed their own form of interpersonal chaos.

Between 1991 through 2015, Community Connections designed and implemented programs to work with individuals in the criminal justice system, women infected with HIV, women who have or are experienc-

ing domestic violence and sexual and physical abuse, children with behavioral and psychological problems, and people with high-intensity
needs. Each of these programs was initially funded by a grant award,
each launched the start of a new clinical department, and each required
that a new treatment model be designed and then empirically tested.
An organization whose initial focus had been clinical case management
for people being deinstitutionalized had now sprouted many tentacles
reaching in multiple directions.

In the area of trauma abuse in particular, Community Connections
became a national leader in designing trauma services and developing a
model for trauma-informed care that was used across the country. Harris eventually wrote three books outlining the Community Connections
trauma model and the organization set up a training department to
orchestrate presentations about the model both locally and nationally
(presenters have now given trainings in forty states).

The values that emboldened Harris and Bergman to start Community Connections in 1984 were unchanged, but the programs designed
to operationalize those values were now many and varied. At times,
some clinical staff began to question whether the values were really
intact and they expressed their concerns that mission creep threatened
to change the very character and culture of Community Connections.

SOMETHING FUNNY HAPPENED ON THE WAY TO THE FUTURE

Harris and Bergman knew how to design clinical programs, how to
make innovative ideas operational, and how to train clinical staff. What
they did not know, however, was how to run an organization.

Over the years, they had referred to Community Connections as a
mental health center, as an organization, as an agency, but never as a
business—until one day, one of the outside financial auditors asked,
"You do know you are a business, don't you?"

How did a psychologist and a social worker who wanted to bring
behavioral health services to marginalized people turn into a business
with all of the issues and problems that all businesses need to solve?
That is what this book is about. Community Connections had been
born, but far from grown.

PERSONAL NOTE FROM MAXINE

In the days before Community Connections first opened, I was predictably nervous.

After all, I had left the security of a "good" government job that came with predictability, benefits, and a secure retirement. And I had taken on considerable professional and financial risk. I remember friends and colleagues asking me if I was certain of my decision. I thought I was.

Then I had a disquieting dream, one that repeated for several days. In the dream, I was a neurosurgeon and was standing in the operating room. I was fully attired in gown, mask, and surgical bonnet, and then, as the nurse was putting on my gloves, I had a terrifying thought, "I was not a neurosurgeon!" I had no training, no knowledge, and I knew nothing of the patient on the table in front of me. I was overcome by a feeling of panic, but then I took some deep breaths, calmed myself down, and went ahead with the surgery. I was flying by the seat of my pants, but I felt that I had no choice but to go forward. The recovery community refers to this as "fake it till you make it."

The analogy to starting Community Connections is fairly obvious. I was scared, I didn't know what to do, and yet I forged ahead anyway.

PUTTING THE COMMUNITY CONNECTIONS STORY AND CULTURE IN CONTEXT

The preceding sections show how Community Connections was animated by a set of core values from its earliest days. Those values included creativity, innovation, a willingness to challenge the status quo, and an element of (what an earlier generation of entrepreneurs would have called) gumption or (what the current generation of entrepreneurs calls) bootstrapping. In this section, we highlight key aspects of the broader literature on organizational culture. As we will discuss, cultures must be aligned internally and externally, and must also be adaptable—to survive and thrive in the face of growth and (often radical) changes in the economic, regulatory, and sociopolitical environment.

WHAT IS ORGANIZATIONAL CULTURE?[5]

Organizational culture is manifested at three levels: assumptions, values, and artifacts. They are often represented as levels of a pyramid or an iceberg, with assumptions being the largest level but also the one that is largely invisible (i.e., below the water line).

The first level, which is least visible, least tangible, includes *employees' underlying assumptions* about how humans behave and how things work in an organization. These assumptions are usually unconscious and so deeply embedded in an organization that they are difficult to articulate—except for newcomers to the organization and/or unless they are violated. Such assumptions often address things like cooperation, collaboration, status, assumptions of positive intent, and so on.

The second level includes the *values that are espoused* in the organization. Such values often appear in recruiting and advertising material; credos; mission, vision, and value statements; codes of conduct; and "culture books." Thus, they are the official representation of the organization to its employees and those outside the organization. Importantly, these values must be supported by policies and practices that consistently reinforce them. If not, those inside and outside the organization view them as either simply empty statements or outright hypocritical ones. In either case, gaps between espoused and enacted values can be especially problematic for an organization.

Into its second decade, Community Connections saw a split in espoused values between new employees (generally recent college graduates) and the more seasoned cohort of employees who had been there with the founders from the very beginning. The younger staff valued teamwork, collaboration, a welcoming work environment, and a mission geared toward social justice. Those who had been with the organization for a while were more focused on transforming the organization into a successful business with a strong balance sheet. This clash between values can, and often did, generate tensions within the organization.

The third level includes the *physical, architectural, and other artifacts* that embody key aspects of the culture. For example, an open office floor plan in which senior leaders share space with other employees can be a physical manifestation of a culture where the free flow of ideas and absence of hierarchy are valued. Conversely, an office with a top-floor executive suite, separate executive elevators, and executive dining areas are artifacts of a very different, more traditional status-oriented culture. In a customer service context, a wide desk or high counter could be an artifact of culture where service is less accessible and friendly. Other artifacts can include things like people's dress, individual workspaces, furniture, and so forth.

Because Community Connections inherited its office space and furnishings, it was sometimes difficult for space and architectural design to match values. The organization espoused certain values, but the space said something very different. Dark mahogany furniture donated by law firms didn't exactly convey a caring, welcoming environment.

WHY SHOULD WE CARE ABOUT ORGANIZATIONAL CULTURE?

Attention to organizational culture exploded between 1975 and 1995 with a profusion of books and articles. Why? First, it was presented as a strongly inertial force that helped explain why so many attempts to change organizations failed—especially the many attempted mergers and restructurings of the 1980s and 1990s. In addition to binding people to the old ways of doing things, it can also blind them to new ways of doing things—limiting change by limiting people's perspective or vision of what's possible or desirable. Second, and more positively, culture can be a source of competitive advantage. When an organization's culture is congruent with employees' values, it helps with recruitment, selection, and retention, and it boosts commitment, job satisfaction, and goal alignment.[6] It also facilitates social control—providing a broader, more effective, more self-reinforcing, and less costly mechanism than contracts or formal controls ever can. Outside the organization, a strong culture can enhance branding and relations with customers because people increasingly buy into the entire culture, not just a product or service. As Community Connections became known as an organization that was willing to try new things, the city and federal government gave Community Connections opportunities that might have been withheld from organizations with a reputation for being more risk averse.

These more positive aspects of culture are the reason that Peter Drucker is reputed to have said "Culture eats strategy for breakfast."[7] In practice, prioritizing culture over strategy, or strategy over culture, is a fool's errand. The *key is creating a culture that aligns with and mutually reinforces other aspects of an organization* (e.g., structure, incentives, work processes, etc.). Since the 1980s, culture and its alignment with other aspects of organizations has emerged at the heart of leading models of organizational design and change (e.g., McKinsey's 7S framework, Nadler and Tushman's congruence model, and Burke and Litwin's change model).[8] When this alignment is in place, culture can be a powerful positive force, which is extremely difficult to copy.

WHAT IS A "STRONG" ORGANIZATIONAL CULTURE?

The strength of an organization's culture can be measured in terms of consensus and intensity. Consensus refers to how widely shared the norms, values, and beliefs are. Intensity refers to how strongly people feel about the norms, values, and beliefs. For example, an organization could have very clear norms about how to dress at work. If you asked a random sample of employees, everyone would be able to describe the dress code in similar terms (even if it isn't formally written down anywhere) and they would all agree that jeans were not acceptable attire in their offices. However, people's feelings about the dress code could be very low intensity. For example, if someone wore jeans to work it would not trigger an outcry, sanctions, or even a comment (despite there being consensus about norms regarding dress). A strong culture has high levels of both consensus and intensity about its norms, values, and beliefs. At Community Connections, everyone agreed and felt very strongly about reaching out and providing services to everyone regardless of their insurance coverage. Conversely, there was passion but not consensus about the role and value of performance evaluations.

IS A STRONG CULTURE DESIRABLE?

When characterized in terms of high consensus and high intensity, a strong culture itself is not desirable. Strong cultures can bind people for good, bad, or evil. Everyone in an organization could agree on its values, but those values could be at odds with other critical internal elements of the organization (e.g., it could be inconsistent with the organization's structure or reward systems); or everyone could agree on the values, but they could be at odds with the current competitive landscape or moral and legal standards; or everyone could agree on the values, but they could be inflexible.

For an organization's culture to be a truly performance-enhancing force—for it to be *strong* in the best sense of the word—it should meet four general tests:

1. Consensus: Is there consensus (among employees, customers, and other key stakeholders) about the organization's core values?
2. Internal Alignment: Is the culture internally aligned (or consistent) with the organization's strategy, people, and systems? How well do the culture-embedding practices support them?
3. External Alignment: Does the culture fit with the competitive environment or landscape in terms of labor supply, customers, and so forth?
4. Adaptability: To what extent can the organization change culture-embedding practices as environments change?

It is this sense of *consensus with adaptability* that is the most challenging aspect of "managing" culture (especially in volatile competitive environments). For example, IBM was well known for its strong culture in the 1970s and 1980s and was the leader in its industry. However, when the external environment shifted from an emphasis on large mainframe computers, IBM's strong culture made it very slow to adapt. The emphasis on large institutional clients, very standardized and formal sales processes, and inflexible reward systems hampered IBM's shift to the PC—and then to Internet-oriented business. It took several CEOs and more than a decade for IBM to reorient its business.

Like almost every start-up growing into organizational adolescence, Community Connections has struggled with just how big it can get without compromising its "family" culture, which many believe made it successful. Some small personal gestures and traditions fell by the wayside as Community Connections grew. At the same time, reimbursements shifted from a casual do-it-yourself approach to one that required signoffs and forms in triplicate.

Organizations like Netflix and Zappos have tried to be very explicit about adapting their culture to fit their evolving business models and the competitive environments in which they operate. Netflix, for example, published (online) a 129-slide deck that describes the seven key aspects of its culture and how it was using a wide variety of talent management policies and processes (hiring, promotion, compensation, vacations, etc.) to embed some nonnegotiable aspects of its culture while retaining the ability to be nimble as it experienced rapid growth. They noted, "The *real* company values, as opposed to the nice-sounding values, are shown by who gets rewarded, promoted, or let go."[9] With an eye toward other organizations' tendency to become sclerotic as they grew, CEO Reid Hastings wrote that Netflix needed "a culture that avoids the rigidity, politics, mediocrity, and complacency that infects most organizations as they grow."[10] There were times at Community Connections, however, when nimble got confused with fickle and staff began to question whether expediency had become the driving value.

The importance of *adaptability* is supported by salient individual examples like IBM and Netflix, but also by large-scale studies. For example, a recent study of public and private high-tech firms in the United States and Europe found that firms with high consensus and high adaptability had net income two to eight times as high as firms with *low consensus and adaptability*.[11]

HOW DO YOU CREATE, CHANGE, OR REINFORCE A CULTURE?

It is common for people to say things like "Before we can do anything around here, we need to change the culture." When an organization seems as dysfunctional as Enron, the culture becomes an all-purpose scapegoat for all of its failings. On one hand, this "culture first" mantra is a useful corrective to earlier attempts at organizational change that ignored the importance of culture (and focused entirely on structural or political approaches). On the other hand, culture cannot be changed directly because it is the accumulated sense of what works or what gets rewarded (or sanctioned). Thus, changing the culture really means changing the underlying assumptions, values, and artifacts in an organization.[12]

In general, there are ten "levers" that can reinforce or change an organization's culture. They include five primary mechanisms by which leaders can make change—many through their own *visible* behavior. The CEO and/or other senior leaders are not the only people who can work these levers, but leaders do have a disproportionate influence on culture through them.

The five *primary culture-embedding mechanisms* are

1. What leaders pay attention to, measure, and control;
2. How leaders react to crises and other critical incidents;
3. How leaders role model, train, and mentor;
4. What gets rewarded, symbolizes status, and leads to promotion; and,
5. What criteria are used for recruitment, selection, and socialization.

Although many people talk about culture being an inertial force and difficult to change, leaders' behavior—as exhibited through these primary mechanisms—has the potential to change culture quickly, especially if changes to the mechanisms are consistent and coherent (e.g., the things that are measured are also the things that leaders devote their time to and are also formally rewarded and used as criteria for recruitment and selection).

At Community Connections, how leaders role model behavior and how they train staff, as well as how they confer status and grant rewards, have been the most powerful of these five primary mechanisms. The first of these—role modeling and training—are spoken about publicly and are a source of pride for the organization. "If you come here, you will learn from the best, with the best, how to be the best." However, the second (promotion) is rarely spoken about explicitly and has been a source of paranoia and accusations of favoritism.

There are also five *secondary culture-embedding mechanisms*, which have a more indirect effect on culture. They are the

1. Formal statements of philosophy, mission, vision, values;
2. Physical design of the work environments, buildings, etc.;
3. Work flow and decision-making processes;
4. Stories, myths, and slogans that describe key people and events; and,
5. Rituals, ceremonies, and celebrations.

Culture develops over time whether we like it or not. That development can be haphazard and organic or leaders can be intentional about creating, changing, or reinforcing their organizations' cultures. Which values leaders emphasize matters, but there is no one right culture or set of values. For some organizations, it is all about creating a culture of innovation. For others, it's all about a culture of reliability, safety, execution, collaboration, sustainability, service excellence, and so forth. The ten embedding mechanisms are not specific to any one culture.

SUGGESTED READINGS

For excellent book-length, but managerially oriented (i.e., nonacademic) treatments of organizational culture, see Edgar Schein, *Corporate Culture Survival Guide* (San Francisco, CA: Jossey-Bass, 2009); Kim S. Cameron and Robert E. Quinn, *Diagnosing and Changing Organizational Culture* (San Francisco, CA: Jossey-Bass, 2011); and Eric Flamholtz and Yvonne Randle, *Corporate Culture: The Ultimate Strategic Asset* (Stanford, CA: Stanford University Press, 2011).

For a good case example, see J. Chatman and V. Chang, "Culture Change at Genentech," *California Management Review* 56, no. 2 (2014): 113–29. For a managerially oriented but academically sound article, see for example, Jennifer A. Chatman, and Sandra Eunyoung Cha, "Leading by Leveraging Culture," *California Management Review* 45, no. 4 (2003): 20–34.

2

HOW TO MAKE AN IDEA COME ALIVE

Inspiration, Thinking It Through, and Making It Happen

All socially driven businesses and creative endeavors start with an idea, an inspiration that drives the decision to open up shop. But a bright idea is not enough. Thinking and implementing are essential to the success of any start-up.

How many good ideas have never gotten beyond that all night discussion that seems like it could change the world? In the clear light of morning, however, the idea either seems not so clever after all, or a realization dawns of just how hard it will be to take that idea and make it real. For many authors, how many titles for books have occurred to them but how very few of those titles actually turn into books? You can't write a book without an idea; and you also can't write a book without a lot of hard work. The same is true for organizations. The following fable tells the story of how one clan takes an idea and turns it into something real.

A FABLE: A TOWER TO REACH THE SKY

One day, as the leaves were turning a golden brown and the squirrels were busy hiding nuts for the coming winter, all the members of the clan gathered together to talk about this and that and to enjoy the cool of the evening. All of a sudden, one young man stood up and looked at his

*fellow clansmen and declared, "I am tired of all of this talking, I am
going to go off and see what I can see." And with that, he looked up into
the sky, saw a bright star, and decided to head off in the direction of the
shining light. He walked for days and days, his eyes fixed on the glow of
the star. And then one night as the dark crept over the horizon, he saw
something rather miraculous—another star, farther in the distance, that
burned with an even brighter, almost fiery light and that shot with
forceful speed across the sky. "How wonderful," he cried into the still
air, "a shooting star; I have seen many stars since the time when I was a
young boy, but I have never seen anything like this before!"*

*And then he began to think, "What if our clan could get so high in
the sky that we could see all of the stars that shoot through the Heavens.
What secrets we might discover. Then we would be the most powerful
clan in the world. Perhaps we might build a watch tower that would
soar as far as the eye could see." With that idea racing through his
mind, he lay down and went to sleep.*

*The next morning the young man rushed off to tell his fellow clans-
men what he had seen. He was flushed with excitement and as he de-
scribed the magic of the shooting star, all who heard his story sat in
awe. "You have truly been touched by the Sky Gods who have granted
you such a wondrous vision," said a wise and old clansman. "Now we
must plan on how to build this tower of which you have spoken."*

*And with that declaration, all of the members of the clan fell asleep
and looked forward with anticipation to thinking of how they would
build the tower that would rise up into the sky. But when they awoke,
the young man who had inspired them to think of a plan was gone. He
had vanished with the morning sun and was on his way to find something else that might be as magical as the shooting star.*

*At first, the clansmen lamented his absence, "What will we do with-
out the young man who inspired us to dream of the tower that would
reach up and touch the sky?" But then a young woman who had not yet
spoken turned to the group and said, "Don't be silly. We can surely
build the tower. Have we not designed our city and the roads that
surround it and the walls that keep us safe from those who would do us
harm? I am sure if we sit together and think hard, we will come up with
a plan to build the tower."*

*And so, for many months, all of the members of the clan sat and
thought and talked about how they might build the tower. At first they*

sat all together in one group, but then smaller groups split off and thought and planned until they came up with many ideas. Each idea was brought back to the wise ones of the clan who debated and changed the plan before sending it back for more thinking. Some of the clan's people were talented thinkers and they were able to analyze the plans. Others were good at testing out different facets of the plan and using their experiments to make changes in the plan. After many months, and much thinking, debating, and testing, the clan's people shook their heads in unison, smiled at one another, and declared: "Now, at last, we have a plan for how to build a strong and tall tower that will reach up to the sky."

While they were rejoicing in their plan, one young man looked up and said, "But wait, we are designers and thinkers and planners; we need builders if we are really to raise the tower to the sky!" Then someone remembered, "Many years ago as we were designing a new wall for our city, we saw some toilers working in the fields. They seemed to be working very hard, but we thought little of them since all they seemed to be doing was gathering wood and stones to build their small homes. But now they may be just what we need, since without some people to build our tower, all we will have are scrolls and scrolls and pages of plans."

With that thought they set out to find the toilers and to ask them if they would take on the task of building the tower. When they found the workers and presented their plan, the oldest of the toilers took the pages that held the carefully drawn plans and showed them to his fellow builders. They studied the plans and turned the pages up and down and then the oldest of the toilers smiled a knowing smile. "Of course we will build your tower, because we are builders after all."

If this story sounds remarkably similar to the process of sending a man to the moon, that is because it is.

In May of 1961, President Kennedy shared a vision and offered a challenge to the nation. In a speech on space travel, he said very clearly and definitively, "I believe this nation should commit itself to landing a man on the Moon and returning him safely to Earth before this decade is out."[1] It was quite a lofty vision, but one that served to inspire a nation to take on a monumental task.

But Kennedy did not stop there. He asked the nation to "do the work and bear the burdens" of making this venture a success. Scientists, engineers, contractors, and technicians would have to work with servicemen and civil servants if this were to happen. Without the brainpower of hundreds, maybe thousands, of people thinking, planning, and designing, the mission would be a failure. He warned the nation that dedication, discipline, and organization would be needed on the part of everyone.

Kennedy spoke like a general contractor who would actually build the spaceship; he called for no work stoppages, no inflated costs of material and talent. He told the nation that there could be no wasteful interagency squabbles or fighting that would impede the completion of the project, nor did he expect massive turnover of personnel. This is what it would take to implement his plan.

INSPIRATION

We can all remember times when we were merely sitting looking out into the distance and something just came to us. It may have been an insight into something we had been working on, or it may have been a time when all the pieces of a puzzle just came together. We may have called it a "bolt from the blue," a flash of insight, or in more religious terms, a "glorious realization."

Regardless of what we call this inspiration, we can easily recognize it. Mozart had it; Salieri did not. Michelangelo had moments of inspiration; his contemporary Alessandro Allori (a relatively unknown artist of the last part of the sixteenth century) did not. And one of Einstein's many moments of inspiration gave the world the theory of relativity.

What are the characteristics of inspiration? An inspiration is an energized idea, an excitement of the mind. It feels and is viewed by others as just having burst through a barrier, a film, a wall, where something veiled becomes clear. But inspiration is not magic. It may seem sudden, but it is the product of a period (sometimes quite lengthy) of seeing, ingesting, being open to experience. Einstein called imagination (what might also be called inspiration) "the highest form of research"—not the research done in a laboratory, but the research of being alive and open in the world.[2] More than that, an inspiration is formed by many things we don't even recognize and may be unable to articulate—the world we live in, the values and worldview we hold, the forces that surround us, the people with whom we converse and debate, the past that has formed the ideas of others.

Inspiration comes to us when we are alone, sometimes in that state between sleeping and waking when we are not weighed down by the cares and obligations of the world. The novelist Saul Bellow advised, "You never have to change anything you got up in the middle of the night to write."[3]

Inspiration often gives the appearance of being quite simple. When we speak an inspiring thought out loud, others may slap their heads and exclaim, "Why didn't I think of that?" But inspiration does not always result in agreement or praise. It may generate confusion, disapproval, or dismissal, especially when inspiration challenges the status quo. What happens when someone declares in the middle of a meeting focused on implementation or concerted problem solving, "Wait, I have a new idea; something just came to me!" The response is often not shared excitement, but rather defensiveness and opposition. Imagine Newton's reacting to Einstein's theory of general relativity, "You can't contradict everything I have worked a lifetime developing."

In a far, far more modest version, staff at a start-up company, committed to working on a new project, might be affronted and antagonistic if a newcomer declared, "I just had a thought about a new way of doing things. Something just clicked." An instance of this occurred at Community Connections when, after many years of designing a new training program, one of the designers herself posited that she had a new idea—one that would overturn the work that had gone on previously. Another woman who had been very invested in the old way of doing things became upset, almost to the point of tears. "You have just invalidated my entire career." Inspiration can be threatening, just as much as it can open new doors and introduce a new and exciting way of doing things.

Perhaps more than anything, inspiration requires an openness to seeing and experiencing things in a different way. Some companies have suggested giving employees blocks of time during which they have no assignment other than to sit and think. Some employees doze off, others get anxious and want to get back to "work," but some let their minds drift, not knowing where they might land. Inspiration brings everything that we perceive and remember and imagine into one integrated whole.

When we breathe, we open our lungs to take in air from the outside. It's oxygen from the outside that keeps us alive. And once the oxygen is inside our bodies it is transformed; we exhale something different, something which may nurture the environment or something which may have a toxic effect. In either case, the process of breathing is called inspiration.

THINKING IT THROUGH

Inspiration is just the beginning of turning an idea into reality; it certainly is not the whole story. Wendell Berry, a twentieth-century writer and activist wrote, "There are, it seems, two muses: the Muse of Inspiration who gives us inarticulate visions and desires and the Muse of Realization, who returns again and again to say 'It is yet more difficult than you thought.'"[4]

Without a period of thinking, discussing, experimenting, and then thinking some more, an inspiration is just a shooting star, brilliant but gone in a flash. Henry Ford had the vision to democratize the automobile and Mark Zuckerberg felt inspired to "make the world more open and connected."[5] But the big inspiration behind Ford Motor Company and Facebook would have died if a period of thinking had not followed, thinking that refined, operationalized, and translated the vision into something that might be implemented. Every inspiration, if it is to make a profound impact on the way we do things, needs to spend some time in what one venture capitalist called an "idea incubator."

The process of thinking through an idea can be done alone, but it is often done in a group, several people working together debating, planning, and challenging one another. "Several people" does not mean everyone in an organization, however. A few heads can be far more thoughtful than one, but dozens of heads spend more time bumping into one another than they do generating productive ideas.

The process of thinking an idea through is more than just brainstorming. A group of people sitting around and talking about anything and everything rarely does more than provide an interesting conversation. During the thinking through phase, ideas are not merely mulled over, but they are tested, put out for others to see, to challenge, to revise, and then to think through all over again.

In their book *Great by Choice,* authors Jim Collins and Morton Hansen talk about firing a number of "bullets" and then seeing which ones have an impact.[6] When we think about a problem, we engage in a lot of trial and error, and we collect data on the outcomes of those experiments. Thinking allows us to have a greater chance of success before we move on to implementing an idea. This is why architects and inventors design prototypes before they commit to a big project.

However, successfully thinking through an idea is not the end of the process. Inspiration and thinking are not sufficient for success—they must be put into operation. In the words of Thomas Jefferson, "Do you want to know who you are? Don't ask. Act! Action will delineate and define you."[7]

MAKING IT HAPPEN

So how do you go about implementing a project? First, you need a plan for how to make it happen. That means having a lead person, somewhat like a general contractor, and a group of people who will do the day-to-day work. But more than that, you need a plan that can be carried out in a series of stages, with an evaluation after the completion of each stage and an opportunity to make additions or corrections as the implementation process proceeds.

It goes without saying that for a plan to be carried out successfully, the participants involved need the requisite skills. Too often people are assigned to make something happen because no one else wants to do it or because they are the first to raise their hands when the project gets announced. But to ensure success, program directors need to specify the skills needed to implement the project and training must be made available to those who require it.

Imagine, for example, that someone is inspired to build an electric car. A group of people discuss the value of such a vehicle and how it might function and who might want to drive it and how it might be marketed, and then another group builds a prototype and evaluates its functionality. Everyone agrees to go forward and build electric cars. But then the critical question arises, just who will do the building? Who is going to take these ideas and translate them into a real object? What skills will they need and how does an organization go about finding those people? Community Connections, as many other similar organizations or businesses have done, fell into the trap of stopping the process at the stage of having an idea and thinking through the process while ignoring the critical importance of a strong implementation team.

Implementers are the doers and not, as they are too often called, the "work horses" of any project, and they should receive the credit they deserve. As Edison pointed out, "Genius is 1 percent inspiration and 99 percent perspiration."[8]

Ideally *Inspiration* should be followed by *Thinking It Through*, which is then completed with *Making It Happen*, but that is not always the case. At Community Connections we have had many missteps in which one of these three critical elements was left out, and unfortunately, far fewer where all were present and neatly aligned. It might be best to start with one case where we got it just right.

CASE STUDY # 1: GETTING IT RIGHT

For many years, Community Connections ran treatment groups designed to serve women who presented with mental health problems, addictive disorders, and struggles raising daughters who seemed to be going down the same path. Despite our belief that we were delivering good services, many of the women who participated in treatment groups continued to engage in abusive relationships, use drugs and alcohol to soothe their distress, and experience uncontrollable emotions. What were we doing wrong? And then, almost in a flash, one of the program leaders realized what was missing. We had all of the separate spokes of the wheel, but we were missing the one critical piece—the hub that connected them all; that hub was sexual and physical abuse. All of these women were the survivors of violent personal trauma and all their destructive behaviors were related to the violent personal trauma that they had suffered.

But having that insight was just the beginning. For almost a year, a group of more than twenty women met weekly to debate, discuss, and at times seriously disagree about how a treatment program might be designed. The discussions went from the theoretical to the very practical. Part of this process involved developing a detailed protocol for service delivery, testing that protocol, and then putting it through a series of revisions before the work group felt that the new treatment was ready to be implemented. Without this period of collaborative thinking, the trauma treatment program would have been nothing more than an interesting idea.

Then came the phase of putting the intervention into practice. Several clinicians were trained to run what came to be called "trauma groups." Their work was evaluated using a fidelity instrument and they were carefully supervised. The cadre of trained clinicians grew as each group leader trained someone else, who trained someone else, and on and on. At the end of five years, trained clinicians were running trauma groups across the country. The trauma treatment model that began with close connections to client and a carefully developed idea for addressing clients' needs was implemented widely and became an industry standard.

But once again, all projects do not result in such a successful outcome. Often one of the three parts of bringing something new across the finish line is missing.

CASE STUDY #2: A MISSING INSPIRATION

At an early point in its history, several of the staff at Community Connections observed that there was no plan for evaluating employee performance. An evaluation tool would make it easier to make fair decisions about promotion, firing, and necessary training. Because we were beginning to think of ourselves as a business, it made sense that we, like most businesses, should have a standard metric for judging employee performance. But an observation that an evaluation protocol was missing was not an inspiration; it was an observation, something like: "It makes sense that every organization should have a method for evaluating the performance of its employees. We don't have one, so we need to find one or design a useful tool for performance evaluation." A plan to evaluate employees is not an inspiration; it is a standard business practice. And an observation that something is missing is not a big bold idea.

Consider how different this process is from the following scenario. "I don't get why staff leave after only one year. Why do they stay for such a short time? Wait, I've got it. Leaving must be related to some combination of performance and skill level of the employee, mixed with employee job satisfaction. Let's evaluate staff performance so we can answer some of the big questions we all care about. Now that's an idea!"

In both of the above cases, senior staff spent months thinking about how to design an evaluation tool, but in the first case they were performing a task and in the second case they were testing a hypothesis. Both groups experimented with different options and the use of different technologies; both discussed and refined their methodologies. But the first group became bogged down in the tediousness of their task. Attendance at meetings dropped off. The group was unable to sustain the interest of their colleagues who were not working directly on the project and their solutions seemed unimaginative and passé. Without an idea to inspire their work, it was not uncommon to hear that dreaded refrain, "Why are we doing this anyway?" And when it came time for implementation, few staff actually filled out the evaluation forms that had taken so long to generate.

The inspiration-driven group, in contrast, had a very different experience. They were looking at evaluation because they wanted to test an interesting and novel idea. Could they learn something about employee tenure by evaluating how frontline staff performed their jobs and how they felt about what they were doing? They designed an evaluation tool only after they met with the staff who were to be evaluated. What would they want to know? How would they like their performance to be evaluated? What did they expect would be done with the evaluations? These ideas allowed for discussion, exchange of ideas, and the eventual crafting of an evaluation tool. The tool was used by managers and was not resented by employees. Both managers and employees used the evaluation data not only to make decisions about promotion and firing, but also to design training initiatives that would make employees do their jobs better and want to stay with the organization longer.

When the process started with an inspiration, the thinking was livelier and the implementation ran more smoothly.

CASE STUDY #3: NO ATTENTION TO THINKING THINGS THROUGH

Several years ago, Community Connections senior staff received feedback from new supervisors that decisions at the organization were being made by only a small group of program managers. This feedback resonated with leadership who felt that they wanted to give all employees a chance to be heard and to have a voice in guiding the organization's course of action and future direction. Using a model that had been initiated at other companies, management designed a series of ongoing meetings that allowed cohorts of staff to meet and discuss issues facing the organization. The groups were called All Minds Matter and junior management staff were asked to be part of individual groups. Everyone thought we had stumbled onto a great idea.

Making the groups happen was relatively easy. Based on program affiliation, staff were invited to attend one of several groups. Each group met either once or twice a month and each consisted of about fifteen members. At first we had lively, albeit unfocused discussions. But then attendance at the groups became somewhat spotty. Conversations seemed to jump from one topic to the next with no continuity from one session to the next. Some members began to ask "what are we supposed to be doing/accomplishing in these meetings?"

In retrospect, we had a good idea and a way to implement that idea, but we had jumped too quickly from the spark of inspiration to the work of making something happen. We didn't spend any time thinking about what exactly we were going to do, what the format of the groups was to be, and how we would evaluate and use some of the suggestions that were generated. Before we began, we did not solicit feedback on whether this was a good idea or what format such an endeavor might take. We didn't start with a pilot group and see how that functioned, nor did we take the time to garner any data from other organizations who had tried to get employee input in just this way. In essence, we had not done our "Thinking" homework.

Using a variant of the old adage, "Look before you leap," it is just as important to "Think before you act."

CASE STUDY #4: INABILITY TO MAKE THINGS HAPPEN

In many instances, a project that began with great expectations ends with great disappointment. That is because organizations are moved by inspiration, spend time thinking through the specifics of how something might be accomplished, but in their enthusiasm often overlook the fact that the idea cannot be brought to fruition. And no amount of thinking it through will make any difference. In the worst-case scenarios, a group may believe that more and more thinking will produce a solution that will result in a successful implementation. But sometimes the resources required to make a good idea a reality are just not there.

Community Connections went through this difficult process for almost two decades as we tried to set up a clinically based housing program for homeless mentally ill adults and families. A member of our senior leadership team, after years of trying to find stable housing for individuals who had been living in shelters or on the streets, had the idea that currently available housing would not be sufficient to solve the crisis of homelessness. As long as people had no treatment for their mental illnesses, no support for their substance addictions, and no meaningful work to occupy their days, they would soon lose any housing that was subsidized and supported by city resources. The idea went something like this: housing was not at the center of the problem, but rather homelessness was the result of a host of other untreated problems. At the time that it was articulated, this reformulation was seen as a novel idea!

With this idea as a starting point, a group of clinical staff designed and piloted a housing program with built-in clinical supports. This plan was validated by other programs in other states and by data from national research studies. The clinicians wrote up their program plan and were ready to get started.

And then reality hit. They had an idea, they had thought it through, but they had no sizeable stock of apartments that was necessary for implementing the plan. The group looked for grants, sought benefactors, and began small with the hope of growing as funds came in. But the struggle was a long and frustrating one. The lesson was clear. Good ideas and serious thinking need real resources if they are to make a change in the status quo.

In retrospect, it is obvious: you need to start with a big idea; you need to go through a process of thinking through the idea; and then you need to find a way to make it all happen. Going forward without one of these three ingredients is never a formula for success. But in the moment, it is often the case that we focus on what is most immediate at the expense of the other elements.

A PERSONAL NOTE FROM MAXINE

In the 1990s I went through a period of intense creativity. I was writing books, helping to nurture Community Connections, serving as a principal investigator on several grants, and seeing clients in a private practice—oh yes, and growing a rather big garden. There were some days when I started at seven and didn't really finish up till nine or ten. As a psychologist and as a woman without children, the thought crossed my mind that I was delivering my creative babies just as fast as I could.

Then, I just stopped—creative menopause, if you will. I continued my role at Community Connections; I taught others what I knew about treatment and I gave lectures designed to help others become better clinicians, but I felt like I had nothing new to create. I didn't have the energy or the drive for something new. When I spoke with my literary agent or with a close friend, I always got the same question. "What are you working on now? When can we expect your next book?" And I always responded in somewhat the same way, "I don't really have anything to say right now," and I didn't want to write something just for the sake of writing. We all know authors who write the same book over and over again, just changing the title as they go along.

But then something happened. I started to have new ideas, one after the other. I knew that they would not all be implemented, but they were starting to grow. I brought other people in on the thinking process. This time I wasn't going to do it alone. And this time, it didn't need to happen so fast.

PUTTING THE INSPIRATION-TO-IMPLEMENTATION PROCESS AT COMMUNITY CONNECTIONS IN CONTEXT

The preceding fable and case studies address concepts that are at the heart of "design thinking"—inspiration, ideation, and implementation. Design thinking is an approach to innovation and human-centered design, as well as something of a movement that was jumpstarted by the award-winning design firm IDEO. Having designed hundreds of products that are now part of the everyday fabric of life in America (from the computer mouse to vibrating toothbrushes to Velcro sneakers), IDEO's approach and design thinking more generally have become the leading models of problem solving and innovation. Although design thinking has its roots in product design by IDEO and other firms, its core principles have also begun to infuse the management of organizations more generally. In this section, we provide additional background and supporting research on design thinking as it applies to challenges faced by Community Connections and organizations like it.

THE ORIGINS OF DESIGN THINKING

Initially, basic human-centered design was applied to physical products. Over time, people began applying it to create better user and customer experiences. In the process, it became known as "design thinking." Sharing some elements with the scientific method and problem-based learning (e.g., all three efforts aim to prevent premature commitment to ideas and active testing of those ideas), design thinking has been extended to treat services, strategies, and systems as design challenges too. Most recently, proponents have been applying its principles to a "well-designed life." Generally, it has seemed most useful in situations with significant tensions, constraints, uncertainty, and ambiguity.

Whether applied to a computer mouse, an organization's strategy, or Community Connections's treatment interventions, design thinking involves two especially important elements:

- A deep, emotional, usually qualitative, almost ethnographic approach to understanding and empathizing with users, customers, clients, and other relevant stakeholders. It is through this deep, empathetic exploration of problems that *inspiration* comes.

- Collaborative generation of ideas (often using brainstorming or brainwriting) and iterative, rapid-cycle prototyping, which involves stakeholders early with "low-resolution" versions of the product or solution so that they have a direct influence on problem framing, data analysis, and solution development. This "solution finding" or *ideation* builds on customer/user based inspiration.

Design thinking's approach to empathizing with users/customers/ stakeholders may involve quantitative data, but it is generally broader than the quantitative "customer research" often resident in organizations' marketing and IT departments and often captured in spreadsheets and user requirements documents. Rather, design thinking tends to use visualization and physical models, drawings, maps, or other more tangible representations of services, processes, strategies, and so forth. Rapid prototyping involves a commitment to active iteration and experimentation, which is captured in organizational mantra's like "Fail Early, Fail Often" (IDEO) and "Demo or Die" (MIT Media Lab). These two elements—through the early and ongoing involvement of stakeholders—make approval of the final product, service, or strategy a formality. Commitment has been engendered all along the way, which makes design-thinking-based *implementation* far easier.

Empirical Evidence for Design Thinking

There are few scientific tests of the effectiveness of design thinking overall,[9] but this is not surprising given design thinking's upstream orientation and the challenge of "testing" an entire approach to anything. In some ways, design thinking is akin to approaches like total quality management (TQM) and Six Sigma in their early days—their assumptions and tools are clear and widely used, but testing their benefits as end-to-end processes is empirically difficult.

However, the examples of successful design thinking and the qualitative evidence for it are voluminous. Its successes are manifest in the many influential products it has created and, more recently, in organizations' effective application of it to services and strategies in corporations like 3M, Toyota, IBM, and SAP and nonprofits like the City of Dublin, Ireland, and Denmark's Good Kitchen.

There is also solid evidence (from more controlled studies) supporting the component parts of design thinking. For example, there is clear evidence for the benefits of user involvement (e.g., in software design) and deep understanding of customer needs and learning from failure. There has also been extensive comparison and scientific testing of different approaches to idea generation and selection. The establishment of academic journals like *Design Issues*, *Design Management Review*, and *The Design Journal* suggest that a more thorough understanding of design thinking's scientific underpinnings is on the way.

The Application of Design Thinking: Core Tools

The suggested readings below provide a longer list and more details about the implementation and use of various tools to support design thinking in organizations, but we provide synopses on five of what we consider the most useful ones here—visualization, experience mapping, assumption testing, rapid prototyping, and customer cocreation.[10] We describe them separately, but they are often most powerful when used in combination.

Visualization. In many ways, visualization facilitates (or is the general form) of many other design thinking tools. Simply put, it takes any information (about customers, products, services, etc.) and depicts it in figures, maps, pictures, and so on. By creating visual images and moving away from the text and numbers that tend to dominate people's work (and this book!), visualization does at least three critical things: (a) it prompts us to reframe things, (b) it allows us to grasp complex information more rapidly, and (c) it appeals to different ways of thinking. As we discuss in chapter 5, reframing is a vitally important step in decision making and problem solving. It ensures that we see things from more than one perspective—and visuals (or 3D objects where possible) facilitate that perspective taking. When we risk drowning in data or text, visuals are often a helpful lifeboat to conceptual clarity. Lastly, good use of visualization appeals to some people's need and tendencies to see something before they can really think it through (others benefit from doing and hearing, so leaving room for them in your process is valuable as well).

Experience mapping. Also known as "journey mapping," this tool involves tracing the experience of customers, clients, or anyone else who interacts with your organization and its products and services. It uses a visual depiction of that experience (for the reasons noted above), and is based on in-depth conversations and observation of the experience. By gathering and depicting the highs and lows of their satisfaction and other emotions while they interact with the organization, experience mapping helps develop a much deeper understanding of the customer experience. That understanding can then more effectively inform the development or refinement of products and services that meet their needs and fit with their existing habits and use patterns.

Assumption testing. This tool recognizes that every new product and service is based on hypotheses about what is valued and what works. Instead of expecting that a product or service will work, it's essential to test the assumptions underlying your hypothesis about why it will work. Imagine a fast casual lunch chain where customers order and pay by phone or iPads in the store. Shortly thereafter, their meals appear almost magically in cubbies for them to grab. It is a combination of online ordering, customization, and vending machine–like delivery. They never see or interact with an employee of the chain. This restaurant's business model is based on the idea that people want speed and don't value personal contact. Before the chain can be successful, it would need to test those assumptions. How much value do customers place on speed? Is it sufficient to outweigh the positive aspects of personal interaction? Does it put low wage workers further into the background in a way that unnerves people enough to outweigh the speed of ordering and delivery? You can imagine the need to test similar assumptions behind all kinds of products and services (e.g., the self-checkout process in grocery stores).

Rapid prototyping. Prototyping is not new in manufacturing, but it has become a staple of design thinking and valuable in more service-oriented organizations as well. It involves the creation of rough physical or visual versions of products and services so that organizations can explore their viability. For physical products, it is easier to see how this can be done. For services, it can involve stories, storyboards, "wireframe" mockups—or actual small-scale delivery of the service or parts of the service. Importantly, it can often also make heavy use of visuals and experience mapping. By developing prototypes, pilot testing them, and iterating, organizations can avoid overcommitting to one particular approach or design and can test assumptions more directly and more rapidly. Visualization is a 2D representation, and more helpful than text or numbers, while a prototype is a more realistic (but still incomplete) 3D representation. Developing these less complete (and often smaller-scale) iterations allows organizations to get feedback sooner and thus to invest less in products or services that may be on the wrong track. Prototypes are especially effective when they involve customers directly.

Customer cocreation. In many ways, customer cocreation is at the heart of design thinking. As noted earlier in this chapter, design thinking is founded on the idea that a deep almost ethnographic understanding of customers or clients is vital for the evolution of an organization's business. Beyond a tool like experience mapping, which draws on observation and interviews, customer cocreation actually involves the customer in a much more active way. It blurs the lines between designer and customer in ways that increase the success rates of the products or services being created. Depending on the stage of the process, customers can be engaged in cocreation with visuals (like storyboards or wire frames) that capture what a service or product will do, look like, and— roughly—feel like. Farther along in the design process, they can involve more tangible prototypes or pilot tests. The best customers for this kind of cocreation are a diverse group (to anticipate the population you intend to serve) who are frustrated with current products/services, but also care about your organization. You want them to be candid and developmental, and to have some intrinsic motivation to help (based on their desire for a better product/service for themselves, not just the compensation that marketers or pollsters traditionally pay focus group participants). Unless the product or service is going to be used in groups, engage customers in cocreation on an individual basis—so they're not reacting based on other customers' reactions. After you're finished, and have involved multiple customers, it's critical to circle back and let them all know how their involvement affected your design and development.

For more details on using these and other design thinking tools, see especially the work of the Stanford "bootcamp" group; Jon Kolko; and Jeanne Liedtka and colleagues as noted in the suggested readings below.

SUGGESTED READINGS

What we've just discussed is necessarily a summary. The good news is that there is a tremendous amount of good work that's been done to make design thinking principles and tools freely accessible. There are also numerous published examples that could be used as motivation or partial guides to employing design thinking in your own organizations.

In terms of specific tools that are helpful in many organizations, there are many valuable resources at www.ideo.com and http://dschool. stanford.edu/use-our-methods/the-bootcamp-bootleg/. There are also excellent book-length resources from Christopher Simmons, *Just Design: Socially Conscious Design for Critical Causes* (Cincinnati, OH: HOW Books, 2010); Colin Ware, *Visual Thinking for Design* (Burlington, MA: Morgan Kaufmann, 2008); and Jon Kolko, *Exposing the Magic of Design: A Practitioner's Guide to the Methods and Theory of Synthesis* (Oxford: Oxford University Press, 2015).

For more real-world examples of design thinking in action, see Tim Brown, *Change by Design* (New York: Harper Business, 2009); and Jeanne Liedtka, Andrew King, and Kevin Bennett, *Solving Problems with Design Thinking: Ten Stories of What Works* (New York: Columbia Business School Press, 2013).

3

POWER, AUTHORITY, AND RESPONSIBILITY

Who's In Charge Around Here?

When mission-driven organizations begin, the last thing they think about is power. Usually there are only a few founders and great consensus on just how things are to be done. But as an organization grows, questions arise as to just who is in charge and who bears responsibility for the success of the organization. This is especially true when the organization grows exponentially with the addition of each new program. Take the example of any start-up organization or business. At the beginning, it is clear that the founder or founders are in charge. The business was, after all, their idea. But then the business starts to grow and new products or services are brought on line, new departments are established, and every department has a manager, and every manager has a team of supervisors who oversee the work.

Now imagine that something big happens: a new opportunity presents itself, the demand for services increases, the need for expensive changes to the organization's infrastructure arises. Who makes the final decision to go forward or to hold back? Obviously, unless the organization functions like a dictatorship—and some do—many people may be involved in gathering data, having discussions, and holding focus groups, but when all is said and done, one person holds the power to decide. The following fable highlights these tensions.

A FABLE: THE MAGIC RING

There once lived a king who had two fine young sons. As the boys grew into men, they drew the praise and admiration of all of the townspeople. Their bond to one another was so strong that it made them appear very special indeed.

One day, they came to their father with a carefully thought out request, "Father, we have lived under your care and guidance all of our lives, but now we are grown men and we are ready to make our own way in the world. We plan to leave the town we have known so well and venture out to build a new city, one that we can rule with all of the strength and wisdom you have taught us."

At first the king took offense at the presumption of his sons. "How could they believe that they might build a city as mighty as his own?" But that was not all that the king felt. He was saddened at the thought of losing his two brave sons, because in his heart he knew that it was right to let them go.

"You are right to want to explore and build a bright new city that will add to the power and breadth of our kingdom. But before you go, I want you to take this magic ring that was given to me by my father and by his father before him. This ring holds great power, so you must handle it with care."

"Father, we will humbly take your blessing and we will promise to be righteous keepers of the ring."

The two brothers set out on their adventure with big plans running through their heads. They knew that there would be many things to do, but they were convinced that together they would be able to build a powerful new city. They worked tirelessly, performing all of the tasks side by side.

After a while, their reputation grew and they had many others who wanted to join their efforts. The more they had to do, however, the more they came to realize that it was just too much to do everything together. They would have to divide the task of ruling into two parts, with each brother assuming authority for making decisions in his part of the new kingdom. As a team, however, just the way they had started, they would jointly hold themselves accountable for the growth of the city.

And so it went for a very long time. And the city prospered. The brothers would look to one another and rejoice in their success. "What more could we want," said the youngest brother. "We have all the power and success we longed for when we left our father's house." But just as the word "power" was uttered, something strange began to happen. The brothers heard a loud rumbling coming from the hills. "Whatever could that be?" cried the brothers in unison.

Then the brothers remembered the ring. The power of the ring had been roused, as if by magic, by the mere mention of its name. "Why, that sound must be coming from our ring; perhaps it is time for us to see the ring once more. I am curious to find out what has happened to it after so many years." So they began climbing to the top of the mountain where they had placed the ring so long ago.

But as they climbed, the brothers grew silent. They were no longer laughing and planning together about their great city; each became lost in his own thoughts of the ring and all the wonderful things he could do with its power. Finally, they reached the spot where the ring lay. As they opened the box that contained the ring, they both gasped at the sparkle and glow of the magic ring. One brother reached for the ring, only to be knocked off balance as the quick hand of his brother grabbed the ring from its box.

"Wait," said the first brother, "the ring is mine to hold." "No," cried the other brother, "I touched the ring first; it belongs to me." The brothers no longer were merely arguing about who had touched the ring first; they now argued over who OWNED the ring. The two brothers, once so very close that they seemed inseparable, now battled and schemed and fought over the ring. Once allies, now enemies. Magic rings have a way of changing things.

Finally, with a sigh of resignation, the first brother took his hand from the ring and conceded, "The ring is yours, my brother, for you are stronger than I am, and you are willing to fight harder for the power of the ring."

The two brothers turned to one another and nodded in agreement. It was time to return to their city; but now, only one carried the ring. Each assumed authority over his part of the kingdom, both continued to have responsibility for the city, but although they never spoke of it again, both knew that the absolute power of the ring would forever and always belong to only one of the brothers.

The fable of the Magic Ring illustrates the complex role that power plays in the evolution of any organization and raises the all-important and somewhat sticky question of who "owns" a business. This dynamic was on public display in the movie *Steve Jobs,* which tells the story of the evolution and growth of the megacompany Apple.[1] Two men, Steve Jobs and Steve Wozniak, shared an idea and a vision that would ultimately change the world of personal computing. But since they had different talents, they granted one another authority over different parts of the business. As the company grew, the partners had to allocate responsibility for a variety of deliverables to several different department heads. All seemed well until a big decision needed to be made about the direction of the company. Wozniak offered a suggestion and without much discussion, Jobs delivered an absolute no. In that moment he demonstrated (for good or ill) what it meant to have power!

In any system, someone needs to have the last word; someone needs to have control over the final decision. Someone needs to believe what Harry Truman meant when he famously said, "The buck stops here."[2] These words and the sign on his desk meant that the power to make decisions was his and, despite consultation and discussion with advisors, it remained his alone.

When we talk about power, we are not merely speaking of the ability to influence decisions but about the right to make decisions. Authority on the other hand is power that has been delegated within the bounds of both time and space. Someone has authority to decide for a certain amount of time within a particular context. For example, when children are left with a babysitter, a parent may say, "You have the authority to make decisions while I am away." The authority is put in context; it is only to be used in the parent's absence and its duration is limited. And in this case, the babysitter certainly would be clear about the limits of his authority. After all, no one gives babysitters power to make lasting or big decisions. But in many organizations the confusion between full, unitary power and limited, contextual authority can be at the root of big problems like employee dissatisfaction, claims of unfairness, and low staff morale.

There have been times over the years when leaders at Community Connections tried to develop, often at the suggestion of a business or management expert, a clear organizational chart intended to map the duties, responsibilities, and reporting structure for all staff. The word "power" was almost always absent from these discussions. Power seems like a scary concept—a word that has no place in a social service agency committed to egalitarian decision making. Power is often the elephant in the room. This is partly a function of how people build or acquire power.

HOW DOES SOMEONE COME TO HAVE POWER?

The most common way that people acquire power is by being present at the beginning. Founders usually hold the power not only because they earned it, but also because there is no one else there to challenge them for it. It is only when others join the organization that the possession of power gets questioned and there have clearly been messy fights in which founders were thrown out of their own companies. But for the most part, founders hold power because it is their company.

In family-owned businesses, power is often passed from one generation to the next; and this may be the case regardless of whether or not the next generation has the skills and the drive necessary to make the business work. In some founder-operated businesses, whether for profit or nonprofit, the founder, other family members, employees, and outside stakeholders may all assume that they know who the next boss will be. While such an arrangement lessens ambiguity and uncertainty, it also may prematurely elevate someone who is not ready for the job. During the Middle Ages, even children who were minors could assume a kingship because they were next in line.

If you believe that you have the power regardless of what you know or what you do, there may be little or no incentive to actually learn how to do the job. After all, the job is yours no matter what you do. Somewhat like the proverbial baseball player who finds himself on third base and thinks he hit a triple. Inherited power also may be demoralizing for other employees who believe they deserve to run the company by virtue of their skills or their seniority. When those employees know that they are stuck in a position of lesser or secondary power, some may opt not to give their best to the business.

At Community Connections, a study of workplace dynamics revealed that the least engaged employees were those in management who knew that the leadership of the organization was not going to pass to them. These employees accepted their positions somewhere in the middle of the organizational chart, which would have been fine since all organizations need people in the middle. However, for some, when they stopped competing, they stopped striving and creating. They adopted an attitude that many citizens, rightly or wrongly, associate with government employees—just hanging around until it's time to collect a pension.

In contrast, a different drama unfolds when a few people, either implicitly or explicitly, do compete for power. Knowing that only one person will ultimately have full power to run the organization, a few people with responsibility begin jockeying for position. This can take the form of acquiring and hoarding information, taking on ever expanding responsibilities as they become available and thereby making themselves indispensable, or reaching for perks and other benefits often limited to the CEO. Such competitions, because they frequently occur behind the scenes, may feel "sneaky" to other employees who watch them being played out.

Overt competition is often the norm in a for-profit business, and it is often the case that the loser of the competition leaves the organization, depriving the business of a competent employee. In nonprofit organizations, however, the culture supports collaboration, not competition, and such a culture promotes the notion that collaboration, and at times prolonged discussion, leads to better performance and better outcomes.

OUR UNEASY RELATIONSHIP WITH POWER ONCE WE HAVE IT

Many people want power. They strive for it, work for it, and even fight for it. But paradoxically, many people don't know what to do with it once they have it. Of course, there are ruthless dictators and controlling parents and tyrannical bosses, but for most people who find themselves in the position of running a start-up or a newly founded social service agency, managing power is something for which they were never trained. So how do such leaders manage their power?

At times, leaders feel that they must avoid using their power until they have more data. Power must be locked up until you have the "key" to open it. At Community Connections, some department heads were always asking for more information. They feared being decisive until they could support their decisions with hard facts. Of course, data are rarely conclusive. And data from different sources can be in conflict and can result in a leader drawing different conclusions. The director of one of our largest departments is known for saying "I don't feel comfortable making that decision without more information." But for him, there is never enough information and important decisions go unmade. At times, leaders believe that the data will make the decision for them. But data are merely one basis for making a decision. Leaders use data, not the other way around.

Some people feel so uneasy being in positions of power that they hide it from themselves and from everyone around them. At Community Connections, the focus has always been on egalitarian leadership. If you walk in, you might well ask, "Who's in charge here?" Everyone, from the CEO to the receptionist, goes by their first name. No one has a secretary and everyone gets her own coffee. The trappings of power are conspicuously absent. In one organization similar to Community Connections, no decision was ever made without a vote of all the employees. Someone who had been hired a month ago had the same vote as the man who had founded the organization.

For some people, wielding power stands in contrast to their personal values and goals. At Community Connections, employees saw themselves as working for the empowerment of those who have been marginalized and disenfranchised. At organizations dedicated to preserving the environment or the lives of endangered species, the goal is to make the world better, not to garner personal power. Even many young for-profit start-up companies want to solve problems and design technology that will make life easier for the average person. These are lofty goals, often at odds with embracing individual power. One does not need to be a Fortune 500 CEO to be willing to exert power; every CEO needs to recognize power and be willing to use it to make important decisions.

Below are some case studies of how power has been viewed, used, and manipulated at Community Connections and—by analogy—at other young organizations.

CASE STUDY #1: DENYING THAT PERSONAL POWER EXISTS

Like the brothers in the fable, cofounders or coleaders in an organization might prefer denying that personal power even exists. The organization grows and is sustained by the belief that no one holds absolute power. "We are just one big happy family, right?" Until a decision needs to be made.

In a social service organization like Community Connections, the issue of power is especially problematic. Almost all staff come from the nonprofit world where power is generally synonymous with greed and tyranny.

One woman, Tony, who eventually became director of one of Community Connections's biggest departments, started her career as a homeless outreach worker. When she was first offered the position of director, she insisted on making it clear that she felt uncomfortable having power over others and making big decisions. In group meetings, Tony, who had always been somewhat reserved, appeared almost frozen. She refused to recognize, much less embrace, her power, often qualifying her statements with offhand and somewhat self-deprecating comments such as "Oh, what do I know anyway?" or "Don't pay attention to what I just said; I wasn't really concentrating." At other times she would look distracted and disengaged.

On one particular occasion, Tony was leading a business meeting when Alex, her second in command, began to roll his eyes, tap his pen on the desk, and whisper to a colleague. Rather than addressing Alex's behavior, Tony became quiet and somewhat withdrawn. Alex then spoke up and took charge of the meeting. Other staff members became a bit uncomfortable but let Alex, the self-appointed leader of the meeting, have his say. After the meeting, Tony confronted Alex about his behavior, but Alex only shrugged and replied, "Well, someone had to take charge." Tony was stressed and frustrated with Alex, but she was unable to acknowledge, much less assume, the power that was rightfully hers. She had denied her power by not using it.

Leaders cannot hide their heads and pretend that power does not exist just because they work for a mission-driven organization or for a young start-up founded by a group of friends. Acknowledging power is part of doing the job. But for some people, power is just plain old scary.

We all remember the look on George Bush's face when he was told that the Twin Towers in New York City had been attacked. His look of shock was apparent, but so also was his look that appeared to be panic. Now we don't know for sure what went through his mind at that moment, but the president certainly looked frightened by the enormous responsibility for the nation's safety that was being thrust upon him.

Sometimes words as well as actions can be used to deny personal power. When asked if they would like the power to make final decisions, some employees steadfastly say no. This is especially true for women who may view their desire for power as being unseemly and who may receive public criticism for what is seen as grasping for power.

In family-run businesses, regardless of how hard an employee works or how well she performs her job, it may seem pointless to voice a desire for power; after all, everyone knows who the next leader will be. Power will be inherited by the next family member in line. The polite answer to the question "Do you want to run this place someday?" is "Not really, and besides I have other plans."

CASE STUDY #2: GIVING OR TRADING POWER AWAY

Let's face it, power can be a burden. Having to make decisions, juggle multiple responsibilities, and take care of hundreds of employees can exhaust even the most stalwart CEO. Leaders are encouraged to master the art of self-care, work with coaches, and delegate responsibilities so that they don't develop "power fatigue" and do harm to the business as well as to themselves. When Shakespeare's Henry IV laments, "Uneasy lies the head that wears a crown," he is speaking of the weight of the throne.[3] In a less poetic voice, he might just as easily have been referring to the strain that comes with having the power of being the CEO.

Shortly after the sudden death of my partner, friend, and cofounder of Community Connections, I felt not only the pain of personal grief, but also the exhaustion of running the company on my own. My partner had skills that I did not possess just as I had talents that were not hers. We used to joke that together we made one whole CEO—like the Roman god Janus, with two faces looking in different directions at the same time. It was hard to imagine how either of us would go forward without our "other half."

In this weakened position, power seemed too heavy a weight and I sought someone who might either share the load or carry it herself. I was, more than likely, looking for a replacement for Helen. And someone came to the rescue, or so I thought.

Cassie was an affable woman in her late thirties who was well respected by most in the organization. Seeing that I was rudderless and likely to make impulsive and perhaps rash decisions, she offered to take over a number of my responsibilities and some of my power. In group meetings, she would often glance in my direction, trying to read my intent. I saw her eager gaze as a desire to make sure that I was not feeling overly burdened, but in fact, to paraphrase Shakespeare once again, "Yon Cassie had a lean and hungry look."[4]

Over the course of several months, Cassie garnered more and more power within the organization. But as I became increasingly rejuvenated, I realized that I wanted my power back. Once traded away, however, most things are difficult to retrieve, and power is especially so. I began to see Cassie as a competitor, not as an ally, and I found myself acting like a fussy child, throwing tantrums, contradicting Cassie's ideas, and slowly withdrawing her authority. I could see myself and my agency spinning out of control. Fortunately, a coach with whom I was working encouraged me to gain a more removed and dispassionate perspective (what he called a view from the balcony) on the organizational dynamic and slowly to take more and more of my power back. Some of it was done in a planned and graceful way and, if I am being honest, some of it was not. The "power" struggle between me and Cassie, even though it ended with my successfully reasserting myself, was costly for me personally and for Community Connections. Relationships were tattered, I lost much personal capital, employees were uncomfortable, and the business floundered for several months. Whenever you give power away, you had better be careful of why you are giving it away, under what circumstances, for how long, and most importantly, to whom.

There is one caveat, however. Sometimes program directors give power away in advance of a planned departure. But planning to give power away can be tricky. Some managers do it too quickly, having the equivalent of a "power yard sale." They leave behind a power vacuum that can easily cause squabbling and temporary dysfunction for the organization. On the other side, it is possible to move too slowly. There is a reason why there are only a few months between an election and the time when a new president takes office. Too long of a transition leaves everyone wondering who really holds the power, the new leader or the person with years of experience. The last thing a new leader wants is to have his predecessor telling him how things used to be.

Somewhat more difficult to discern than the giving away of power is the trading away of power, but you need go no further than the Old Testament to discover an example of trading away power. As the eldest son of Isaac, Esau was poised to inherit the wealth and power possessed by his family. But after a day of strenuous hunting, Esau was exhausted and hungry. When offered the chance, he willingly and without really thinking traded his birthright to his younger brother for a bowl of porridge. As twenty-first-century readers of the Bible, we may find this trade hardly seems like an astute move, but at Community Connections and at many other small or medium-sized nonprofit businesses, trading away power happens more often than one might think.

Women, for example, may find themselves inclined to trade power for friendship or some semblance of friendship. Hard research and qualitative studies, for example, suggest that women are more relational than men.[5] They want to feel liked and accepted by the people they work with. At Community Connections, leadership made a point of using first names to address one another. Even during a job interview, the interviewer, a member of the leadership team, frequently made a conscious effort to level the playing field by saying to the applicant, "Please call me Mark. If I am going to use your first name you can certainly use mine." A message that says "We are equals, we will be colleagues, maybe we will even be friends." While such casual interaction is in sync with the friendly ethos of the organization, its primary purpose may be to satisfy the relational needs of its leaders.

In this effort to be friendly, Community Connections went further than just using first names. The co-CEOs baked cookies, handed out prizes for good performance, and sent birthday cards and occasionally even flowers to employees, implying a personal relationship. All of this behavior made employees believe that Community Connections was a friendly place to work and that its leaders were nurturing and caring. What it also did, however, was result in the leaders trading away some of their power.

When leaders adhere to policies and procedures, rather than breaking rules for "their friends," they can be seen as mean and uncaring.

Chatting casually about personal struggles and making hard choices can cause others to see leaders as weak and vulnerable. At Community Connections, for example, where the co-CEOs acted like "good old Helen and that's just Maxine," they were treated with disrespect. They learned that once power is traded away, it is very hard to get it back. Staff can end up feeling confused, duped, and even betrayed. Once the toothpaste is squeezed out of the tube, only a magician can get it back in.

Bosses can be friendly, they can express concern and make employees feel cared about, but in the end they are bosses who have the final say in decisions. They should not be seduced into trading away their legitimate power.

CASE STUDY #3: TAKING ADVANTAGE OF PERSONAL POWER

Power can be intoxicating and, like a strong drink, it can make us dizzy, causing us to feel that we are bigger and stronger than we actually are. Regrettably, at Community Connections and other similar organizations, the overuse of power often takes the form of bullying. Young leaders in particular have little experience in being in positions of power and think that the only way to manifest power is to flex their muscles publically. Abraham Lincoln wisely cautioned that if you wanted to measure someone's character, "See what they do when you give them power."[6]

Early in our history, I recall asking a young staff person for a favor. He looked at me, tilted his head and looked startled, and then dismissed my request. My first response was to be dumbfounded, but my second response was to get angry. "Doesn't he realize who he is talking to? After all, I am the BOSS." I barked some critical and shaming words in his direction and stormed off to my office. And I did this within hearing range of some other staff who were milling around near the conference room. I was badly shaken as I entered my office in another part of the building.

I learned an important lesson that day. Power does not give you the right to disrespect another person. It does not condone shaming another person. Real power does not require a battering ram. My actions had several consequences. I felt embarrassed by my behavior and offered an apology, which was only perfunctorily accepted. I had clearly crossed a line. The young employee felt beaten up and subsequently left the organization, and I had revealed a particularly ugly part of myself. Others had heard my outburst and now looked at me with a certain measure of fear and distrust. Shaming another person is not power; it is what one can get away with when one has power. Margaret Thatcher, the former prime minister of England, wisely said, "Being powerful is like being a lady. If you have to tell people you are, you aren't."[7]

CASE STUDY #4: CONFUSING POWER WITH AUTHORITY

When people are given authority, they often mistakenly believe that they have absolute power. Take the example of Roxanna, a talented clinician who had worked at Community Connections for almost six years, since the start of her career. She seemed like a natural choice when the agency decided to open a new program for troubled youth. The CEO gave Roxanna the *authority* to design the residential program and to hire the staff who would be responsible for the daily operations. Roxanna, however, did not have the *power* to increase the program's budget or to decide how its success would be judged. Those big decisions would be made elsewhere. The CEO was clear that Roxanna's authority was limited, both in time and in scope.

That was where the first mistakes were made and where the confusion between authority and power began. Roxanna, her staff, and the children in the program were all unclear as to who was in charge. When there were big decisions to be made or a crisis that needed to be resolved, people asked to see the boss.

Even though she and her staff and other employees in the organization had been told that she was in charge of the program, she felt as if that was not really the case. She had authority, but no power (and in that perception, she was correct). Roxanna felt the eye of management looking over her shoulder. She saw what she believed to be her power slipping away. But Roxanna had never been told the difference between power and authority. Those with power had delegated authority to her. She had not lost her power; she never had any to begin with. The story had a very sad ending. Roxanna felt that she had been used and duped by senior management. The leaders felt that Roxanna had not performed her job well and the youth in the program felt unprotected and many of them left treatment prematurely.

Before concluding, there are two other concepts that need attention because they are often used when talking about power and authority: responsibility and accountability. Whether it is in a business or in one's everyday personal life, things need to get done. Responsibility is like having a job description (the activities, tasks, behaviors that a person is charged with accomplishing). Someone needs to be responsible for "making the trains run on time." Unfortunately, this level of responsibility, although vital for running any operation, is limited and can be easily disrespected. That is because the responsibility of action is rarely coupled with either authority or power.

At Community Connections, and other similar nonprofit organizations, most of the direct services are performed by entry-level clinicians. Their day-to-day activities are spelled out in a job description with little room for variation. They are the actors who deliver the services for which Community Connections is known, and they and their supervisors are responsible for making sure those services are delivered competently and according to protocol. When giving people responsibilities, though, managers also need to give them the training and the resources to do the job. Frontline workers often complain that they are being asked to "make bricks without straw"—to assume more responsibilities with fewer resources and little or no recognition.

Finally, accountability hovers over power, authority, and responsibility. We look to the accountable person when we want to know "Whose bright idea was this anyway?" Who gets the credit? Who deserves the blame? When someone makes a serious clinical or financial error at Community Connections, they may feel remorseful or apologetic. They may try to remedy the mistake, but ultimately, I am accountable for the consequences of their actions. As I have been heard to say, "Be careful what you do, because I'll be the one getting sued!"

In first-generation founder-run businesses, the founder is literally the owner. If things are not run correctly and the business fails, the founder will be held accountable. As a result, founders may be reluctant to delegate important tasks, may not trust the advice of team members, and may have difficulty devising a clear plan for succession. As a founder of Community Connections, I have been accused of doing more than a little looking over the shoulders of my employees, making sure that everything is done just right. Too much pressure to hold one person ultimately accountable can be bad for your health, but it can also be bad for the health of your business.

A PERSONAL NOTE FROM MAXINE

Only recently have I seen the CEO title applied to directors of nonprofit agencies like Community Connections. It took me several years, in fact until after the death of my partner, to have the letters CEO printed on my business card. My doorplate still bears my professional degree, Maxine Harris PhD, and when asked what position I hold at Community Connections, I merely say that I am the director. Now some of this may be my personal discomfort, some of it may be that in the practice/ professional world, we are more comfortable displaying our academic credentials, but I think discomfort at being thought of as the boss also plays into the mix.

Shortly after Community Connections opened, a young employee gave me a coffee mug with the logo "She Who Must Be Obeyed" printed prominently on the side. As she handed me the mug, the young woman was tentative and somewhat intimidated, clearly unsure as to how I might receive her gift. I felt flattered, seeing the inscription as a compliment. A male colleague sitting across the room began to laugh. Three different reactions; three different perspectives; all commentaries on power. I knew that the moniker "She Who Must Be Obeyed" was used by Rumpole of the Bailey in reference to his wife, but I suspect that was not the real origin of the phrase. [8]

I discovered that in 1887, the writer H. Rider Haggard published the fantasy novel *She*. One of the protagonists in the story is Ayesha ("She Who Must Be Obeyed"). [9] Ayesha is a sorceress from an ancient and otherworldly kingdom who wields enormous and almost unimaginable power: the power to heal, to raise the dead, to know the minds of her subjects, and of course, the power of immortality. In the end of the novel, however, the sorceress steps into the flame of immortality one time too many, losing all of her life preserving power as she crumples to the ground, an ancient and shriveled hag, no longer "She Who Must Be

Obeyed." *She* is a frightening and ominous tale, which might just capture some of the struggles and dangers that go with having and using power.

PUTTING LEADERSHIP, POWER, AND RELATED CONCEPTS AT COMMUNITY CONNECTIONS IN CONTEXT

As noted earlier in the chapter, the word "power" often carries many negative connotations—power grabbing, power struggle, power trip, power play, and of course, Lord Acton's "power tends to corrupt and absolute power corrupts absolutely."[10] Dating back three centuries, society has also had an uneasy relationship with ambition or the desire for advancement and power. As Jeffrey Pfeffer has written, people like to believe that the world is just and fair, so ambitious striving for power is unnecessary if not outright unseemly.[11] Part of the negativity is a function of language and the word itself. Before addressing the dynamics of shared leadership, which were central for Community Connections, we address the language of power and other concepts related to leadership and leading.

Leadership or *leading* is a *process* of social influence to guide, structure, and facilitate behaviors, activities, and relationships toward the achievement of shared goals through cooperation and free will, not force. It may be exerted by those in formal positions of authority, or those without it. When exerted by those without formal authority, leadership is generally based on moral, social, intellectual, informational, or other forms of power. Leadership is most effective when it rests not solely on formal authority but also on some combination of other forms of power.

As the definition above indicates, influence, power, authority, responsibility, and accountability are all central to leadership, decision making, and control. They are also often equated or conflated, which is problematic because a lack of clarity regarding these terms often portends a lack of clear roles and "rules of engagement."

Influence is a process by which we change circumstances or behavior. For example, parents can (try to) influence their children's behavior and supervisors can try to influence the staff in their unit to follow procedures more closely.

In contrast, *power* is the *potential* or *capacity* to *influence* other people, groups, or events. Power can be conferred or based on one's position (in which case it's called "authority"), or it can be based on other factors, including personal characteristics (e.g., charisma), social connections, status, information, expertise, resources (i.e., "power of the purse"), and so on. In either case, power rests on differences—differences in position, differences in status, differences in access to resources, differences in respect. For example, if I am the youngest person on a team, my power might be based mainly on my technical expertise. I would have limited connections in the organization, I might not be especially charismatic, and I wouldn't have any budget.

As noted earlier in the chapter, *authority* is power that is formally conferred. Authority is the formal, legitimate (usually position based, institutionalized, and/or legal) right to make decisions, direct people's actions, commit resources, and so forth. Authority is generally delegated formally or conferred based on one's position. It comes with a responsibility for your actions and the actions and resources that you direct (or fail to direct). It is a subset of power.

For example, we may have some power over our children, but that power changes as they age, and we may or may not be successful in our attempts to use it. Until they reach age eighteen, we have both informal power and formal power (or authority) over them. After they turn eighteen, we no longer have formal power or authority over them. Fortunately or unfortunately, society still sees those children as partially my *responsibility*. If children go off the rails and get in trouble, even if they're twenty-five, the community (or society more broadly) will view the parents as (at least partially) responsible.

Responsibility is the duty (to followers, peers, superiors, and/or society) to carry out a task satisfactorily. It comes with consequences (formal or informal) for failure to complete that task. Responsibility can be assigned by others or assumed based on one's own promises or circumstances. For example, we're responsible for our children's welfare. We can delegate that responsibility to others for short periods of time, but we're responsible (and ultimately *accountable*) for their welfare.

Accountability is a sense of obligation when people must answer for their actions (or inactions) and accept the positive or negative consequences. Those consequences can be legal or social/informal. Account-ability is generally something that cannot be delegated. If we're ac-countable, we must account for our activities, accept responsibility for them, and disclose the results in a transparent manner. We are all ultimately accountable for our own actions, though others may some-times be implicated for influencing those actions.

For example, former Volkswagen CEO Martin Winterkorn may not have been directly responsible for the emissions control systems scandal with VW's diesel engines, but he was accountable for the actions of VW employees. When it became clear that VW had cheated to pass emis-sions tests, Winterkorn was quickly held accountable in the court of public opinion, and he resigned. Ultimately, he may also be held ac-countable in courts of law.

POWER, DECISION MAKING, AND SHARED LEADERSHIP

Power and shared leadership featured prominently in the Community Connections story. They also feature prominently in many (if not most) new organizations. Founders of organizations face three core types of dilemmas—about roles, relationships, and rewards.[12] Role dilemmas are fundamentally about power and decision making, and they are con-siderably more difficult when the cofounders have relatively similar skills.

Early on—during the days when there is more work than arms, legs, and brains to do it—many cofounders occupy overlapping roles. Over time, a clearer division of labor can support better accountability and a more careful match between strengths and roles. Ideally, founders and founding team members build deliberate consideration about (and flex-ibility into) their roles so that they can evolve thoughtfully and inten-tionally as the organization evolves.

Whether founding teams are explicit about decision-making struc-tures and processes, there is nearly always some tension between being democratic, inclusive, and consensus driven or being clear, direct, and more autocratic. The latter generally includes a single person who is accountable for making the final decisions—and is usually a faster ap-proach to decision making. In dynamic environments, although consid-eration of multiple points of view is important, research suggests that

centralized decision making (under relatively dominant CEOs) is associated with decreases in firm performance.[13] More egalitarian approaches are more common when founders have similar skill sets and
when neither carries the official CEO title—either by design or because
they've avoided the sticky question of titles altogether. There is a tendency among many founders to just "punt" on difficult conversations
regarding roles and titles (not to mention relationships and rewards).

Co-CEOs occur occasionally—as with Oracle, Whole Foods, Chipo-
tle, and RIM, the company behind Blackberry phones. Unfortunately,
they do not have a particularly good track record. As one study put the
conundrum of such shared leadership models: is it *dual* or *duel*?[14] The
approach has only been studied in a handful of social service agencies,
where it seems to be adopted more frequently by female leaders, but
there is a deeper base of knowledge based on co-CEOs of corporations.
For example, a 2014 study by Krause et al., of seventy-one co-CEO
pairs of publicly traded U.S. companies, showed that firm performance
increased as the power gap between the co-CEOs increased.[15] In other
words, performance improved as the leadership structure moved away
from a "shared command" approach to a "unity of command" approach.
This was true except when the gap between the two co-CEOs' power
was extremely large. Co-CEOs also seem to be associated with a less
independent board structure and fewer advising directors.[16] If done
well, this can be balanced by the co-CEOs' mutual monitoring of each
other, but for large organizations it is a significant risk.

The paradox is that most leaders conclude that the CEO role is best
held by one person, but they also begin their organizations with relatively egalitarian and loosely specified roles that often include a substantial dose of shared leadership. This was true in the early days of
Community Connections, until roles and responsibilities at the top became more clearly defined and divided. With that clearer division
comes the potential to make decisions more rapidly.

In its early days, Community Connections operated with a shared
approach to leadership. Formally, there were two directors, not initially
referred to as CEOs. Over time, although those titles remained in effect, specific responsibilities and accountability for aspects of Community Connections's operations diverged. Reflecting the two founders'
strengths and preferences, Maxine assumed responsibility for clinical
operations and Helen assumed responsibility for administrative opera-

tions. As they assumed these roles, it became clearer within the organization who was accountable for what, but not everyone was open to the coleadership approach. In fact, titles were not formalized until a grantor required that they be listed on a grant proposal. The initial submission named co-CEOs, but it was sent back with the request that a single CEO be listed, which caused considerable upheaval.

The generally positive effects of more clearly defined roles at Community Connections are consistent with the research indicating that organizational performance is generally enhanced when there is some distinction in the power held by cofounders or coleaders. With the exception of parenting, having two leaders with equally shared power, responsibility, and accountability is often a recipe for inefficiency and conflict. At the end of the day, for an organization's sake, knowing "where the buck stops" on any given issue helps staff move forward.

SUGGESTED READINGS

For more on the dynamics and performance implications of different forms of shared leadership and our often uncomfortable relationship with power, see Craig L. Pearce and Jay A. Conger, *Shared Leadership: Framing the Hows and Whys of Leadership* (Thousand Oaks, CA: Sage Publications, 2002); Jeffrey Pfeffer, *Power* (New York: Harper Business, 2010), and—especially in start-up contexts—Noam Wasserman, *The Founder's Dilemmas* (Princeton, NJ: Princeton University Press, 2012).

4

HIRING

People to Help With the Work

One of the most important, even essential, tasks for any business is hiring and retaining talented employees. This can prove especially difficult for nonprofit businesses that are mission driven to the point of caring far more about new hires' passion and commitment than their skill and training. The dilemma becomes even more powerful in founder-run, nonprofit businesses (often staffed initially with friends and family) where issues of mission and commitment are confounded by relational concerns and a strong desire to "make everyone happy."

It may only take a few people to start an organization, but it takes many more to actually run it. So how do you go about the process of hiring new staff? Do you design the job and then hire the best person, or do you find good people and then let them create their own job? These were not questions with simple answers as Community Connections moved into its second stage of growth.

A FABLE: THE CLOTHING IN THE CHEST

It had been a very cold winter. Many of the villagers were unused to the freezing temperatures and did not have any clothing to keep them warm when the winds howled and blew circles in the fallen snow. "Oh, how cold I am!" cried one of the older and most respected of those who were huddled together in the center of town. "I would take any clothing that would keep me warm, ANY clothing at all." The other villagers nodded their heads in agreement, but no one had any idea as to how they might find garments to keep them warm throughout the remainder of the long winter.

At the same time, the daughter of a wealthy merchant was sitting in front of a warm fire in her large house. You would have thought that she would be quite content to be so cozy and snug, but this young girl was quite bored. "What shall I do?" she asked out loud to no one in particular. "I will be quite frustrated if I cannot find anything to do on all of these cold afternoons." In search of something to hold her attention, she wandered throughout the many rooms of her large house. Just when she thought she had seen all there was to see, she stumbled upon a hidden staircase that led to an attic that she had never been to before. In the center of the attic room she spied a very old chest that had been covered with all sorts of beautiful blankets. "I must open this chest," she declared. "I know I will find something wonderful inside to keep me busy for all the long days of this cold winter."

And sure enough, she was right. The chest contained all sorts of clothing. Clothing for women and girls, clothing for men and boys. There were coats and sweaters, leggings and dresses, and all varieties of gloves and mittens and well knitted hats. "What a treasure," the girl exclaimed, "I will take all of these lovely things and sort them into orderly piles, then those who are in need of warm clothing can come and take their pick." She worked for days and many long hours, but finally, she was done with her task. She went to the center of town and found the respected elder and told him what she had found and what she had done. At first he looked at her with some skepticism. "Was this rich young girl playing a cruel joke on all of the huddled and freezing villagers?" But after a while he was convinced of her sincerity and turned to the waiting crowd. "We have been blessed with great good fortune. The daughter from the big house has found warm clothing for us all."

Just as they heard the elder's words, the villagers began to scream and holler and push, racing each other to the front of the big house. The elder's cries to wait and to choose wisely from the piles of warm clothing went unheard or unheeded. Every man, woman, and child began grab-

bing and pulling at the stacks of clothing that had once been organized into neat and carefully sized piles.

One tall woman grabbed a very small dress and pulled it over her head with much tugging and straining. Another husky fellow found a pair of slim pants and a fitted shirt and squeezed himself into both, and still another very small girl, who was shivering in the cold, found the biggest dress she could see and stepped right into the large opening intended for her head.

When all of the villagers had chosen new clothing and had dressed themselves for the cold winter, they turned and thanked the young girl and began to run and hurry back to their own homes. But as they made their way, many of them noticed something strange. The big woman with the small dress could only take very small steps because her legs felt bound together. And the man with the tight shirt and pants had to hold his arms and legs out as if he were a scarecrow. The young girl with the big dress fell down again and again, tripping over the long hem of her new dress.

When the villagers finally arrived at the center of the town, they were greeted by the wise elder who looked at them all and shook his head. "My dear friends," he intoned, "it's not enough to have some clothing, you only stay comfortable if you have the right clothing." The villagers had learned a hard lesson, and next time they would choose more wisely.

The fable of the "Clothing in the Chest" suggests why hiring is such a complicated process. Both the employer and the employee need to know exactly what they want and what they are looking for. The villagers just want to be warm; they really don't seem to care what clothing they put on to get them to that goal. Similarly, some prospective hires just want a job, any job, just so long as they get a paycheck to help them pay the rent.

The girl in the story isn't really invested in the goal of keeping the villagers warm. She is just occupying herself by giving the clothing away. Her satisfaction comes from knowing that she has emptied the chest, not from making good matches for individual villagers. In the same way, naive or inexperienced employers can fill a position just so they can say that it has been filled, not because a good match between a job and an employee has been made.

Over the years, Community Connections has had to hire several thousand (taking turnover into account) employees. This is a sizeable number for a clinical organization that began with only three people. Although we have made a large number of "right" choices, we have also made more than our share of mistakes. Like the villagers in the fable, we have placed the wrong people in jobs that did not fit and we have placed the right people in jobs that kept them too tightly constrained. At our worst, like the apocryphal tale about the emperor with no clothes, we placed people in jobs that really did not exist at all.

THE PROCESS OF HIRING

The process of hiring should begin with a series of careful assessments. Like most things, success demands that you know what you want, how to get it, and how to tell if you've gotten what you set out to find in the first place.

Assessing the Organization

What is often missing in a start-up nonprofit business is an organizational chart. While this may be unthinkable in a large, established business, it is usually the routine in a start-up; after all, what is the need for an organizational chart when the business consists of two or three partners who find themselves doing a little bit of everything?

But first, what is an organizational chart and why should it play an important role in hiring decisions? A chart lays out the employment structure of the business. Going down vertically, the chart lays out a hierarchical structure. Quite simply, "who reports to whom?" Just who is my boss? As the business grows, the chart gets bigger and longer. There are directors and departments and supervisors and line staff, to say nothing of relationships on the horizontal axis across departments between directors and others. If you are now totally confused, you are feeling just what founders of growing nonprofit organizations feel. At one point, the chart at Community Connections grew so big that we had to lay it out on the conference room floor, expanding across several pieces of paper.

This confusing jumble occurs because nonprofit start-ups begin with people, not with charts. As a nonprofit begins to embrace its identity as a business, it makes sense to draw an organizational chart to determine who should be hired next, to fill what function, and to whom they will report. But the old culture dies hard, and the pull to "just hire" people when you need more staff is strong. Like so many founders (including those at Community Connections), it is very easy to take that organizational chart, crumple it into a ball, and toss it into the trash can.

But before going to that extreme, it is wise to acknowledge the critical function of an organizational chart, namely, that it provides much needed structure to the organization and to the hiring process.

Defining the Job

A job description outlines just what constitutes the activities of the job, what skills are required, and what qualifications are needed. Just as importantly, a job description places the job within the organizational chart. It tells an employee where he or she fits. Do you report to the CEO, to one of the directors, or to someone who operates as part of the support staff? These placements on the organizational chart define an individual's decision-making role, her power, and her connection to the mission of the organization.

For most people, a clear and well-defined job description is essential for good performance. Some may even feel quite anxious when they do not know just what they are supposed to do. But for others, too much specificity feels constricting and is viewed as a limit to innovation. In fact, some businesses are experimenting with giving some employees a "sand box" in which to innovate and try out new ideas—just the opposite of a tight job description. So we need job descriptions, but we also need the power to go outside them when it makes sense.

Assessing the Individual

Understanding the job and what it requires is the first step toward making a good hiring match. But assessing the individual is equally important. The girl in the fable needed to make a careful assessment of the clothing that was in the chest, but she also needed to assess the villagers. Who was tall? Who was big and who was small? Who was young? And all the other variables that allow us to make distinctions among people. The field of human resources provides a number of ways of evaluating individuals—from testing their skills and looking at their work history and past performances, to having them be interviewed by supervisors and peers, or placing them in a work situation and seeing how they perform.

The problem, however, is that most beginning nonprofits rarely use these strategies. Too much process seems too expensive, organizations are too small to have a full-fledged Human Resources (HR) department, and quite honestly, most start-up nonprofits don't trust standardized tests. So what do they do? They "trust their gut," which means overvaluing likability—the "would you like to have a beer with this person" test. It also means falling victim to the "is this person similar to me" fallacy. Is this person the same age as me? Did they go to the same college? Are they from the same background, race, or ethnicity? Are they the same gender? Since none of these variables has anything to do with the ability to perform a job well, it is no wonder that so many young nonprofits suffer from high turnover rates.

There is yet another stumbling block that makes assessing the prospective employee difficult, and that is our pursuit of a fantasy, an elusive "it" that we think will allow one candidate to rise above others. This quality can be something we call passion, or curiosity, or creativity. The problem with all of these is that they are difficult to measure because they are nearly impossible to define. If I ask, "What is passion?" and all you can reply is "I know it when I see it," then we don't have real criteria for assessing whom to hire.

Evaluating the Choice

Now you understand your organization; you have defined the job and assessed the individual. How do you know if you have made the right choice? This puts us in the world of performance assessment.

There are hundreds of performance assessment tools that measure a range of outcomes. It seems obvious that performance should be tied to goals, but the smaller the organization, the vaguer the goals may be. For many small nonprofits the goal is merely to survive. As time passes and an organization meets goal number one, larger goals get set and goals are assigned to particular individuals. And the more quantifiable the goal, the easier it is to measure.

All of this sounds quite rational and makes good sense, but the more procedures start to sound like what happens in a business, the harder they are to implement in a mission-driven nonprofit organization. You hear the complaints again and again, "We're here to help people, or solve problems, or create new ways of doing things, not to fill out personnel assessments." Try telling someone who joined the organization to help homeless veterans that she has to spend time filling out evaluation forms!

But evaluation of employees is essential to making sure the job gets done and the mission is accomplished. Evaluations help with making other decisions such as promotions and bonuses and lateral moves to new departments. They also help with decisions about firing people.

In nonprofits, especially human service organizations, the word "fire" is almost a dirty word. Rather than reflecting a mismatch between employee and job or employee and organization, it is seen as a failure, on the part of the supervisor, the team, and more specifically, the employee. And since supervisors do not want to seem unfair, the decision to fire an employee often drags out far longer than it should, with a string of employee improvement plans and coaching sessions. It is clearly a stretch for many people who run nonprofit businesses to view firing as a normal and healthy part of the hiring process. Like the villagers in the fable, however, sometimes you just need to take the ill-fitting clothes off and wait for another opportunity.

Understanding some of the factors that should be considered when hiring employees goes a long way toward making the right hiring decision. But we all know that even the best knowledge is not enough to prevent mistakes. Here are some of the misguided ways in which all-important hiring decisions got made at Community Connections.

CASE STUDY #1: HIRING FROM THE OUTSIDE

Hiring had always posed a problem for Community Connections. Once you get past hiring your friends, you need a method for hiring new staff. Over the years a rather byzantine process evolved for hiring at Community Connections. An ad was posted; a resume came in and it was vetted first by a clinical supervisor, then by the CEO. Acceptable resumes were then sent to a clinical department where a second vetting process took place. The candidate would ultimately have a personal meeting with the CEO where a final decision to hire or not to hire was made. The whole process could take as long as three weeks; during which time clients who were slated to become part of the new hire's caseload had to wait to be served, some very good applicants took jobs with other organizations, and many of the involved parties found it difficult to track where we were in the hiring process.

It was clear that we had a problem with the way we hired new frontline clinical staff, but we seemed stuck when it came to fixing the problem.

Part of the reason that such an awkward process persisted was that each of the interviewers along the way had an interest in keeping things just the way they were. Responsibility for hiring carried a certain status within the organization—interviewers got to know all the new hires and form relationships. Being left out might give others the impression that the supervisor was just a cog in the wheel and not an important part of the hiring process.

Changing the process might also mean turning authority for hiring over to the HR department; yet people were skeptical that since the HR department was not made up of staff with clinical backgrounds, they would not know how to evaluate clinicians. The fear was that HR would end up hiring candidates with good resumes but without the heart to be caring clinicians. This was one of those gut beliefs that persisted despite the absence of any empirical evidence. It took years to alter the hiring process and senior supervisors clung to the belief that the old way, cumbersome as it was, must be the right way to do things since "it had always been done that way."

CASE STUDY #2: HASTY HIRING

For Community Connections, the decision to hire additional staff was often in response to an immediate and sometimes unanticipated need. In the mid-1990s, the organization applied for and was awarded a large federal grant. Before the funders had announced the grant awards, leaders were reluctant to hire the fifteen new staff who would need to begin delivering the services. There was a feeling of hope, without any certainty. So we waited, knowing that when the awards were announced, and if we were successful, we would have to scramble to hire the necessary staff quickly.

Once Community Connections was granted one of the awards, the process of hiring began. Yet, after several weeks, with internal and external pressure mounting, Community Connections was still short several clinicians. At that point, consideration turned to some less skilled applicants.

Brandy was one of those individuals and so she was hired for a position for which she was only somewhat qualified. On the plus side, she did have the necessary education for the position, and she was also very willing to learn. Most important, she was a positive person who brought a sense of optimism that everything would work out well on the new project.

However, she also had several deficits, some of which were obvious at the time of hiring, others which emerged as she began the job. Although she had taken the right courses in college and graduate school, she had very few clinical skills and almost no experience working with a very challenging group of homeless, traumatized, and addicted women. When Brandy felt overwhelmed by a clinical problem, she felt too intimidated to ask for help from a supervisor and instead withdrew into her office. She would also substitute social conversations with her colleagues for actually spending time engaging with the clients. Her positive personality, which had been one of the reasons for hiring her in the first place, now became a cover for not doing the work.

In addition to her overall deficits, Brandy was poorly suited for the particular job for which she was hired. Because the job was part of a federal grant, the tasks to be performed were quite specific. Clinicians needed to meet with clients a certain number of times per week, they needed to learn how to run clinical groups, and they needed to log a certain number of hours each week doing outreach to noncompliant clients. Such a job required someone with clinical savvy, creative thinking, and a willingness to reach out to supervisors for help. None of these was a strong asset for this employee.

After well over a year of trying to help Brandy fit into the job for which she was hired, the head of the HR department, Brandy's supervisor, and Brandy herself made a decision for Brandy to transfer to another department within the organization. Her skills were no better matched to the new job, but at least it was a chance for a new beginning. Eager to make a good impression and to experience a measure of professional success, Brandy began her new job with the same sense of optimism and good spirit that she had demonstrated when she had begun the first position. But once again, her performance fell to a marginal level. Paradoxically, she never did well, but she never did quite poorly enough to actually be fired. One improvement plan followed another and Brandy managed to improve just enough to meet the minimum standard. Through all of this, she managed to maintain a friendly attitude and continued to be liked, at least superficially, by her colleagues.

After one more equally unsuccessful transfer to yet another department, the supervisor, having decided that it was time for Brandy to move on, resolved to try a different strategy. Instead of resorting to the previous option of improvement plans and meetings with HR, the supervisor began to counsel Brandy that her own professional needs were not being well served by continuing to work at Community Connections. She had not received any promotions, she had failed to pass an exam for professional licensure, and many of her old colleagues had moved on. What the supervisor did not tell her was that she was no longer seen as a friendly colleague. Her colleagues felt resentful that while they had to work hard, she seemed to be getting a pass. The supervisor himself was frustrated since her poor performance pulled down the productivity scores for his entire department.

It was clearly time for her to move on, but in the absence of a fireable offense, the supervisor spent almost eighteen months cajoling Brandy into submitting her resignation. There was a clear feeling of relief when she finally did. She was given a warm good-bye party and was quickly hired by another organization where the job requirements were much lower. Her current position at Community Connections was then filled with someone who had the clinical qualifications for the job and the right education, as well as the positive personality that had been seen as Brandy's greatest asset. Brandy had been hired for all the wrong reasons. We needed someone who could fill the position quickly. Everyone liked Brandy. And we mistakenly thought that with the right training, we could give Brandy the skills she needed.

CASE STUDY #3: INCORRECT INTERNAL MATCH

In the early 1990s, about ten years after we began our business, we found ourselves with the good fortune of having several strong young employees. One woman, Judy, had worked as a lead clinician on a government-funded demonstration and evaluation project and had shown outstanding clinical skills. She engaged well with her clients and formed lasting relationships, and she worked effectively and collaboratively within the context of a clinical team. As well, Judy was comfortable with the slow and incremental rate of change that characterizes work with seriously mentally ill, impoverished, and sometimes homeless individuals. Her paperwork was adequate but she had trouble completing it on time, in part because she much preferred spending time with clients.

After five years of doing this work, however, she felt ready for a new challenge—an opportunity for professional development. Since we did not want to lose her, we looked around the agency for other job opportunities. At around this same time, our intake and assessment department was under pressure to expand its capacity. Every new client needed an initial intake, done according to a specified format. Individuals also required a reassessment every three to six months. Adding almost eighty new clients per month meant that we needed a highly trained cadre of licensed professionals who could perform these tasks.

The intake/assessment job required that the professional meet people quickly, get all the relevant information in only two hours, and after writing the report, hand off the client to another clinician who would begin the actual clinical intervention. Three to six months later, an assessment needed to be written on all clients and the intake/assessment workers would be responsible for doing and writing those assessments, again using a specified template. We assumed that since Judy had been an outstanding clinician herself, she would understand the clinical issues and be able to perform the job well.

The intake/assessment job, however, required a very different set of skills. Intake workers had to meet people quickly, form a superficial relationship, and begin asking questions. Since the billing codes only allowed for a two-hour meeting, the worker would have to wrap up the meeting and complete the report within that time frame. Each member of the intake staff worked independently and only called on her colleagues if she needed someone to see extra clients waiting for an appointment. The work had to be done quickly and the paperwork needed to be done according to protocol with no room for creativity.

After some coaxing, Judy transferred from her position as lead clinician to one as intake clinician. It should also be noted that the intake position came with a higher salary, allowed the staff person to work more regular hours so that she could leave to pick up her young child, and had no line authority over others that might require writing personnel evaluations, nor were there hiring and firing responsibilities.

Not surprisingly, this particular transfer proved to be a disaster. After almost a year, Judy admitted defeat and left Community Connections. She felt demoralized and far less self-confident than when she had accepted the new position. The department suffered because of a backlog of new referrals, decreased billings, and depressed morale. No one likes to work alongside an unhappy colleague.

As we did a postmortem on just what had happened, we were able to see and articulate a series of highly operative but unspoken, or worse yet, unknown assumptions. First, we assumed that any good employee could be trained to do any job. We assumed that a job merely consisted of a collection of tasks that required a set of skills to be successfully completed. In the case of Judy, she was a bright woman and surely she would be able to learn the tasks that were necessary for completing the intake form, meeting the client, asking a set of questions, and writing those answers into a predesigned template.

We assumed the tasks required certain skills: the ability to write clearly, knowledge of the *Diagnostic and Statistical Manual*, the ability to complete a task in a timely manner, and the ability to set and follow a schedule for completing the tasks. We also thought that both skills and tasks could be taught. And on that front we were correct. Judy learned the tasks quickly and was instructed and coached to develop the needed skills. Where we made our mistake, however, was in assuming that mastering tasks and skills was all there was to performing a job. We neglected to take into account temperament and preference. Judy just wasn't cut out to be an intake/assessment worker. She thrived on interaction; she was, in the vernacular, a people person. She was curious about people and wanted to take time to really get to know another person. A simple intake assessment did not answer all of her questions. She preferred to spend time getting to know the person who lived underneath the symptoms. And so she chafed at having to stick to an externally imposed timeline; she liked setting her own schedule and working at her own pace.

We made a second mistake when we assumed that Judy's main reason for taking the new job is that she believed that she would love the work. But love of the work is not the only reason, or in some cases the main reason, why people accept jobs. Judy was motivated by wanting a promotion, the monetary reward, a predictable schedule, and avoiding supervisory responsibility. Again and again we overlooked the multitude of non-work-related reasons for accepting a job: the need for professional development, the desire to be close to a spouse who is going to school or working in DC, money to pay off student loans, and the list goes on.

Perhaps the most amusing example of this occurred when a young man came into my office for a job interview. He lounged on my couch, seemed to daydream when I asked him questions, and acted as if he could not wait for the interview to end. When I asked him why he was here since he did not seem to want the job, he replied quite candidly. "I just graduated from college and my mother says she'll kill me if I don't look for a job." It is no wonder that some employees are not a good fit for the job they seem to be seeking. After all, they were never accepting the job; they were accepting the perks that went along with that job.

CASE STUDY #4: CREATING A JOB

Over the years, as Community Connections grew, there were many employees who had reached the top of the career ladder in their particular department. Miso, in particular, had been an excellent manager of a small division. She would be a logical choice to head up her department, but the existing head had no intention of vacating his position. Conversations with the current head about his other job opportunities proved fruitless. He felt comfortable in his current level of responsibility, did a good job running his department, and had no intention of leaving.

This left Miso with no obvious place to go. There were no other positions in other departments and no prospects of any vacancies any time soon. She was doing an excellent job in her current position, but

Miso felt bored, wanted a new challenge, and longed for a promotion. The only option seemed to be for her to leave Community Connections and work for another organization. Because we did not want to lose her or her talents, we made her a rather unusual offer. The agency's growth presented so many opportunities and while we did not have a specific job for her, we gave her the opportunity to create her own job.

At first, Miso was tremendously enthusiastic. What an opportunity! There were no constraints on the job except her own imagination. For a while, she spent her time surveying other departments, asking questions, and thinking about what she could do. Her informal investigation had the unanticipated effect of making other employees nervous. Was she there as an evaluator? Was she there to take their jobs? Why was she being given this special opportunity? Rumors began to fly and Miso, once friendly and well liked, found herself being avoided and excluded.

But that was not the worst of the experiment. Miso struggled to construct a project for herself. She floundered and became depressed at her inability to construct a job that either she or the organization would find useful. Finally she came up with a proposal, but the position she envisioned was neither creative nor expansive. It was a small administrative task not worthy of the salary she was receiving. After several months, with both the employee and the organization questioning the wisdom of this plan to allow Miso to create her job with total independence, Miso resigned. She left feeling demoralized, questioning her own skills and her professional competence. Somewhat surprising, senior management felt relieved and somewhat chagrined by her departure. What had started as a chance to create something new and exciting for the organization and something rewarding and self-esteem boosting for Miso ended in failure.

A PERSONAL NOTE FROM MAXINE

As I thought more about this daunting task of finding and hiring the right person for a job, I was reminded of my very first job as a professional. I arrived at the job eager for my first assignment, but my employer had no assignment for me. He merely told me to go to one of the hospital wards and see what I might do. I wandered onto the ward, and introduced myself to the nursing staff who grumbled in my direction before they got on with their duties. I attempted to talk with a few clients, but most of them were either overmedicated or psychotic and could not or would not engage in conversation. A few even told me to "Get the hell off the ward!" and find something useful to do. That experience was enough to send me running to the library. I read, and hid, and plotted my next move to find another job. After about three or four months of this routine, I relaxed enough to start thinking. Sure enough I did have ideas, things I could do that might not have been tried before, and I began to envision a new way of thinking about psychiatric problems that might shift the focus of my practice and that of others. I came very close to feeling both the anxiety and the fear of chaos. If I had succumbed, there would be no Community Connections.

PUTTING HIRING AT COMMUNITY CONNECTIONS IN CONTEXT

Talent management has become a huge object of organizations' effort and an industry unto itself—with companies providing preentry screening to exit and alumni services. Along the way, a substantial body of research and management advice has emerged to address each stage in the process. In the best talent management programs, these stages are well integrated with each other and carefully connected to the organization's goals, strategy, structure, and culture. In this chapter, we explore the selection or hiring stage (recognizing that good selection cannot be done in isolation from the steps that come before or after it).

In this chapter we focus on external hires, recognizing that internal promotions are extremely important as well.[1] In chapter 8, near the other end of the talent management process, we address succession planning.

A VERY BRIEF AND NECESSARILY PARTIAL HISTORY OF HIRING

Systematic testing of potential employees dates back to at least the seventh-century Chinese Civil Service exams.[2] Over the course of the last 150 years, hiring has evolved from early unscientific methods (graphology, physiognomy, phrenology, astrology, etc.) to a more rigorous and scientifically studied range of approaches (including testing for factors such as personality, integrity, cognitive ability, intelligence/s, work styles; using assessment centers, situational judgment tests, and other approaches of simulated work; biographical data; references and recommendations; interviews; and trial periods). The last fifty years of research regarding these approaches has developed in parallel with legal challenges to hiring, promotion, and compensation practices; pressure from rapidly growing and globalizing organizations, as well as rapidly changing technology; a periodic undersupply of qualified employees (and the associated "wars for talent"); and the steady development of more powerful, less costly statistical techniques.

Over the last half century, strategic human resource management and industrial-organizational psychology have also emerged as significant subfields in management and psychology, with their own professional organizations (SHRM and SIOP), codes of conduct, and publications. Modern, systematic, and evidence-based approaches to hiring have been tested and refined largely by members of those two organizations and the affiliated Academy of Management. When surveyed about what aspects of human resources research all practicing managers should know, the members of the field's leading editorial boards listed selection-related items as four of the top six.[3]

WHAT ARE WE HIRING FOR?

Assessing the effectiveness of any approach to hiring requires specifying criteria. Hiring could be oriented toward time to hire, cost of hiring, recruits' perceptions of the process, the employee's subsequent performance, retention, adaptability, leadership potential, organizational citizenship behavior (scholar-speak for "going above and beyond"), team- and unit-level outcomes (not just individual ones), service excellence, or many other desired outcomes.[4] For example, in the service sector (an organization like Community Connections would be an apt example) and in other areas where customer service is critically important, retention might be an especially important criterion by which to design a hiring system. Effective hiring also has broad and extremely valuable follow-on effects, with excellent recruiting associated with three and a half times more revenue growth and two times more profit margin than for other employers.[5]

REMEMBER WHO'S SELECTING WHOM

The hiring process is fundamentally bidirectional and involves both selection and sales—that is, the potential employee selling the employer on their talent, appropriateness for the position, and fit with the organization. In addition, the employer also needs to be selling the potential employee on the desirability of the position and organization. As mentioned in chapter 1, selection is one place where a strong culture can play a valuable role—by sending important signals to potential employees about what it's like to work there. For employees who don't perceive a fit, the strong culture triggers valuable self-selection of the process. For employees who like the culture, a strong one can begin binding them to the organization before they are even offered a job.[6] Because Community Connections, for example, is in a metropolitan area where there are several strong academic programs, new graduates have several job opportunities and the process of selling applicants on the organization often takes center stage.

TOP FIVE EVIDENCE-BASED BEST PRACTICES FOR HIRING

Of all areas of human resources or talent management, hiring is the one with the greatest potential for research to further affect practice. The research is strong and a manager's tendency to follow that research lags other areas (like training or compensation practices). In general, less than 40 percent of managers agree with staffing-related research findings, despite the robustness of those findings. Whereas there are knowing-doing gaps in some areas of management and organizational behavior, there appears to be a believing gap when it comes to evidence-based staffing practices. For example, approximately 85 percent of managers falsely believe that conscientiousness predicts job performance better than intelligence.[7] At Community Connections issues of loyalty to the organization and passion for the work often trumped more objective measures.

Despite seeming intuitive, the following five best practices are widely underutilized. Organizations that defy the norm can expect more success in their hiring.

1. *Evaluate candidates based on samples of their work.* Although they can be costly to develop and implement, there is no better way to screen candidates than by assessing samples of their work—be it actual work done for the company (done during internships or probationary periods) or simulations of actual work. Large employers like Google are increasingly assessing how well applicants can do tasks that mimic the ones they would have to do on the job (coding or solving problems)— and relying less on interviews.[8] Work samples rated by trained raters with clear rating guides explain roughly 29 percent of variance in performance. At Community Connections applicants were often rated on their performance in the last job rather on the skills they would need to do the next job.

2. *Select for intelligence and conscientiousness.* This may sound like an insanely obvious piece of advice, but it is one that has generally been dismissed by practicing HR managers. This dismissal is partly due to concerns about how to test fairly and effectively for intelligence without triggering lawsuits. It is also due to a series of deeply entrenched negative stereotypes about intelligence (e.g., intelligent people are impractical, arrogant, socially inept). However, "intelligence is virtually uncorrelated with such personality traits as conscientiousness, agreeableness, and emotional stability."[9] For lower-level jobs, intelligence (or general mental ability, GMA) and conscientiousness are approximately equal in terms of how well they predict future performance. For higher-level, more complex jobs, intelligence explains roughly 25 percent of variance in performance, while conscientiousness explains 9 percent. Unlike more expensive work samples or structured interviews, there are low-cost, well-validated tests of intelligence and conscientiousness that are not off-putting to applicants. In situations where adverse impact on certain demographic groups is a particular concern, simulation interviews (rather than tests) can be also used to gauge intelligence. Community Connections often confused scholastic degree with intelligence and focused almost exclusively on analytical rather than emotional intel-

ligence. Mistakes were made when very smart people lacked the can-do spirit necessary to working with very disabled individuals.

3. *Use structured interview programs.* Again, many may see this as another obvious practice, but research clearly shows that people prefer to rely on gut instinct and perceptions of chemistry with potential employees, despite the clear evidence that structured selection processes are more effective. This was particularly true at Community Connections where so many of the people hired for new positions were staff who had been with the organization for a long time. They were considered "part of the family" and structured interviews seemed superfluous. Structured interviews use a standard set of questions—ideally asked by multiple interviewers—and behavioral anchors for their responses. They can be used to gauge a variety of cognitive and interpersonal skills, abilities, leadership styles, and other factors of interest to many employers. Although more costly to develop and implement than tests, they also explain roughly 25 percent of the variance in future performance.[10] The challenge to acting on this best practice is the general preference for free-wheeling interviews that interviewers believe are better at assessing fit, interpersonal skills, general likability, and so on, but structured interviews are approximately three times more effective than unstructured interviews.[11] The preference for unstructured interviews is especially strong at organizations like Community Connections where senior staff believe themselves to have strong people skills.

4. *Provide candidates with realistic job previews.* This simple practice helps candidates assess their fit in the organization and is one of the best predictors of retention. Employers should level with applicants about the job and organization—warts and all. At Community Connections, interviewers have been clear that the work is not done in the office but out in the field, and they add the phrase, "It's down and dirty out there."

5. *Obsess over details and first impressions.* Especially for in-demand candidates who may have other options, impressions formed about the organization early in the recruitment process are especially important. So is recruiter warmth. Those who have contact with applicants should be honest about the position and organization, but their interpersonal skills have a large positive impact on applicants' job choices.[12]

THE FUTURE IS HERE

The future of hiring will undoubtedly involve greater reliance on technology (for outreach, recruiting, screening, and every other step in the process) and more in-depth use of people analytics to connect the hiring process to performance measures. Firms like Google, Facebook, and LinkedIn have already changed the field in dramatic ways—and will likely continue to do so. But for founder-run organizations like Community Connections, the move into the future poses to be a problem.

This simple list of questions will help you audit your hiring process and assess the extent to which it follows evidence-based best practices.[13]

1. Are we considering combinations of tools to achieve the highest validity and lowest adverse impact?
2. Have we considered how our ordering of tools affects validity and adverse impact?
3. Are we clear on the criteria we are using to assess our process (job performance, retention, etc.)?
4. Are we providing applicants with the specific information they desire?
5. Have we selected recruiters who are warm and friendly?
6. Is appropriate attention being given to early recruitment activities?
7. Do we solicit feedback from applicants on their satisfaction with the process, including those to whom we made offers and those we didn't?
8. Do we have evidence that selection procedures are job related?
9. Is the selection process consistently administered?
10. Does the process allow for some two-way communication?

SUGGESTED READINGS

For two accessibly written treatments of selection and talent management more broadly, see Claudio Fernández-Aráoz's two excellent books, *It's Not the How or the What But the Who: Succeed by Sur-*

rounding Yourself with the Best (Boston, MA: Harvard Business Review Press, 2014) and *Great People Decisions: Why They Matter So Much, Why They Are So Hard, and How You Can Master Them* (Hoboken, NJ: Wiley, 2007). Also see James Breaugh, *Recruiting and Attracting Talent* (Alexandria, VA: SHRM, 2016); and A. M. Ryan and N. T. Tippins's excellent review, "Attracting and Selecting: What Psychological Research Tells Us," *Human Resource Management* 43 (2004): 305–18.

5

BARRIERS TO SOLVING PROBLEMS

There Must Be a Way Around This

Any business needs to have a series of goals in order to move forward with accomplishing its mission. And anything that gets in the way of reaching those goals is considered a problem. Since internal circumstances and external context are both fluid and constantly changing, it is not surprising that most organizations must contend with all shapes and sizes of problems.

There is no such thing as a problem-free business. Some problems are a natural and expected part of growth. Others arise at choice points when pros and cons need to be weighed and decisions need to be made. Some are driven by changes in the world outside of the business. And some are the result of a faulty solution to a prior problem. Regardless of how a problem arises, an organization that cannot solve the many problems it inevitably must face cannot survive.

But organizations, especially new ones, do not come with an easy-to-read manual for solving problems, or a magic wand that wipes problems away in an instant. The process of identifying and solving problems is complicated and often difficult and there are many barriers that one encounters on the way to a successful solution. Remember the board games we all played as children. There were wrong turns, cards that told you to go back to Go and start all over again, and even landing spots where you were ordered to go directly to jail. All were barriers to reaching the ultimate goal of winning the game.

In the following fables, we tell two tales about problem solving. The first deals with the array of problems you might encounter on the way to a solution. The second addresses how your perspective affects how you see, define, and frame problems.

FABLE #1: CROSSING THE WOODS

For many years, the town of York had been known as the safest town for miles around. There was no fighting or stealing and the children could play without anyone worrying that there would be a problem. In fact, the children did not even hear the word "problem" until they reached the age of thirteen. And when that special age arrived, each child, who was now considered a young man or a young woman, would meet with the elders of York in a tent on the edge of town.

"You have enjoyed the safety of our town for all the years of your life, but now we must tell you something very important. Safety ends at the edge of town. If you choose to enter the darkness of the forest, we cannot promise that you will not encounter all manner of problems."

When they heard this warning, all of the children sat up straight and nodded their heads, for they had no desire to risk the safety they had enjoyed all of their lives—except for one rebellious and very curious young woman. Although she nodded her head like all the others, she secretly thought, "This forest sounds quite interesting, perhaps the elders are just trying to hoard its treasures for themselves. I will wait a while and then I will explore the forest for myself."

The young woman waited for several days, until she could control her curiosity no longer. "I will slip into the forest after dark; I am sure I will be able to overcome any problems I might encounter since I am brave and clever and strong." So she packed a small bag and walked to the edge of town.

As she stepped into the darkness of the forest, she saw what looked like a small pond, but when she got closer, she realized that it was no more than a puddle of rainwater left from last week's storm. "I hope this is not the problem the elders were talking about, because I can cross this pond quite easily." And so she did, without making even a single splash.

Confident that she could now manage any problem she might encounter, the young woman continued on her way, until she stumbled on a big tree trunk that had fallen right in the middle of the path. "Oh, dear, this problem seems far more difficult to solve than the last one. I must sit and think for a while. And so she did. While she was pondering what to do, she saw a narrow trail that wrapped around the far end of the fallen tree. As she poked her nose around the back of the tree, she saw that she could get around the trunk with very little trouble at all. "Whew," she said, as she let out a great sigh of relief. "I didn't really want to crawl over that tree trunk. I might have scraped my knee or even broken a bone, but now I don't have to find a way over at all!"

As she proceeded deeper into the forest, the young woman encountered many more obstacles to overcome, but because she was indeed brave and clever and strong, she found a way to handle each of them.

"I am not sure what the elders were talking about," she said to herself. "There have surely been problems to solve and obstacles to overcome, but none has been so difficult that I have been unable to make my way, and at times my journey has been quite fun. I think my adventure through the forest is almost done." But although the young woman was just about done with the forest, the forest was not quite done with her.

Up ahead, she could see where three small trails branched off the main path: one led to a beautiful field of flowers; the second led to a sunlit waterfall, and the third led to a meadow of tall grasses that swayed in the breeze. As she pondered whether she should go exploring along one of these paths, she heard a stern but clear voice calling from the forest behind her, "You are not here to pick flowers or to see waterfalls or to sit in the tall grasses. You are here to conquer the difficulties that have made it hard for others to cross the forest."

She thought to herself, "I am not sure where it came from, but I am glad I could hear the sounds of warning. I might have made a great mistake if I had let myself be distracted by the small trails. I must be careful to walk with determination down the main path."

But as she continued to walk, her step was more tentative and cautious than before. She had to admit that she could not have solved the last problem on her own. She had needed help from the voice of the forest. What if the next problem (for surely there would be a next problem) was just too hard for her to solve at all?

Solving problems is one of the primary responsibilities of any CEO and senior leadership team. First, problems must be identified and accurately labeled. The girl in the story realizes that she can cross the water when she accurately labels it as a puddle and not as a pond. Misdiagnosing the problem might have led to a wrong solution and perhaps time-consuming and frustrating effort. Imagine if she had continued to see the puddle as a pond, she might have spent hours or even days building a boat to help her cross to the other side.

But solving problems requires more than making a decision and acting quickly. It also requires stopping, thinking, and weighing options. This more deliberate process helps the girl solve her second problem of passing the big tree on the path.

As she proceeds, the young woman sees the value of taking advice and avoiding or limiting distractions, but she comes to the realization that there will always be problems to solve. It is just the nature of crossing the forest, or in this case, building a business.

When Edmund Wilson, one of the most renowned literary critics of the twentieth century, wrote, "No two persons ever read the same book," he was not referring to the obvious fact that there are millions of books in the world.[1] Rather, he was echoing the voices of many who maintain that whether it is a book, a painting, or a problem, we are only capable of seeing things through the lens of our own perspective. Naturally, when two people look at a problem, they see it through very different lenses.

Perspective not only reflects who we are and where we sit in relation to others, it also goes to the core of determining what we see. Abraham Lincoln said, "We can complain because rose bushes have thorns, or rejoice because thorn bushes have roses."[2] It all depends on your perspective and it is impossible to solve a problem without a perspective of your own. Oscar Wilde wasn't just being witty when he declared, "The man who sees both sides of a question is the man who sees absolutely nothing at all."[3] The following fable highlights the role of perspective in problem solving.

FABLE #2: THE TIGER AND THE VEGETABLE POT

One summer day, while a group of children were playing on the edge of the village green, they spotted a tiger lying in the deep grass. Periodically, the tiger would lift his head, shake it from side to side, and begin pacing from one end of the green grass to the other. The children watched the tiger for a while and then one young boy said, "That tiger must be very hungry; he has not eaten in all the time we have seen him."

"You are right!" cried a very small girl who needed to stand on her tiptoes just to see the tiger. He looks very skinny and I am sure he would cross the field if he were not so weak."

"Yes, I see what you mean," said the young boy. "We must find some way to feed him."

Then the oldest girl in the group said in a very knowing voice, "We will make him a pot of our very best soup. We will use all the vegetables from this year's harvest and we will flavor it with herbs and spices to make it ever so good. And when the tiger has eaten it all, he will feel very full and strong."

"Yes! Yes!" cried all of the children at once. "We must make our soup right now!"

While the children were chopping and making their soup, the tiger gazed longingly across the village green. "Oh, how I wish I could see my wife and our little cubs. If it were not for these children making soup right in the middle of the green, I would have an easy path across the village. I have been hunting and climbing trees and running in the fields, but now I am ready to return to my family. What ever can I do?" he moaned in a low voice that sounded almost like a faint growl. As he contemplated his dilemma, the tiger rolled over, twitched his ears, and thought some more about how he might get home. Then he stood on his hind legs, pawed the air, and thrust himself into the air and across the green, knocking the pot of soup as he ran.

The children looked at their wonderful soup, now spilled and making the grass all wet and soppy. "The tiger must have been so wild with hunger that he could not wait for us to finish our soup," they lamented. "We must be faster the next time we see a hungry tiger." The tiger meanwhile was home in his den but feeling somewhat exhausted from his long run. "The next time I am returning home from a long journey, I must be careful to avoid silly children who know nothing about the ways of tigers."

The problem seen by the children is quite different from the one perceived by the tiger. They bring their own knowledge and past experience to the task of solving the problem of "the hungry tiger." It should not be surprising that they arrive at different solutions because they are perceiving and then solving different problems. The children want to feed what they perceive to be a hungry tiger and the tiger wants to get past the children so that he can make his way home. What we see determines what we call a problem and therefore what we arrive at as a solution.

Operating from different points of view is not the only difficulty that leaders of organizations encounter when things seem to be stalled and problems seem to be blocking the way of progress. There are other less obvious factors that present barriers to successful problem solving. The following case studies highlight some of the most prominent ones.

CASE STUDY #1: NOT FRAMING THE PROBLEM WELL

Like many social service agencies that engage clients with serious mental health issues, people with addictions, individuals who have been homeless and possibly incarcerated, the safety of staff was a predictable concern at Community Connections. For some time, staff and clients at Community Connections complained and expressed concern that the environment in which they worked was not safe. One woman reported that her mother drove by the organization's offices to "check out the neighborhood" before she gave her daughter the green light to accept a job. Examples like these caused us to conclude that people were concerned with their physical safety. And framing the problem in this way, we set out to put a number of safety measures in place.

We gave all employees identification badges with a magnetic chip to help them get through locked doors. We rearranged our waiting room where large crowds and hidden spaces had been a cause for concern; we hired two security guards to patrol the main building and we even considered installing a metal detector, an option that went against one of our core values of being an open, community-based organization.

And yet the belief persisted that Community Connections was not a safe place to work (despite the fact that we had experienced no robberies, assaults of staff, or break-ins in twenty years).

Then something changed. One of our senior managers suggested that perhaps it was not physical safety that was the concern, but rather the problem was that people did not *feel* safe. Once you frame the problem as deriving from a *feeling* of unsafety, a whole different set of solutions emerges. People feel safer when they are part of a caring community, when they have the sense that they know and trust their coworkers and that those coworkers have their backs. To that end, we planned a number of "meet and greet" events. We had ice cream socials, went to baseball games together, and generally got to know one another not just as colleagues but as people. By increasing the sense of belonging that individuals felt toward the organization, we also increased their feelings of safety.

Additionally, we did one other thing: we instituted monthly safety rounds, meetings in which staff members could share events during which they had felt unsafe. In these meetings they could get support, feedback, and suggestions from senior staff. The perception that management actually cared about their well-being made staff *feel* safer.

By changing the frame from physical safety to emotional or perceived safety, we were able to solve the problem of "Community Connections is not a safe place to work."

CASE STUDY #2: SEEING ONLY YOUR PART OF THE ELEPHANT

As it approached its fourth decade, Community Connections experienced a revenue shortfall. Quite simply, we were spending more money than we were bringing in. At one point, the shortfall required using a line of credit slightly more than 10 percent of the organization's annual budget. This was clearly a problem that needed to be solved quickly, but different groups of staff members held different points of view about how the problem should be tackled. Those differing perspectives seem to have grown from the ways in which Community Connections had been paid over the years. One department had been supported by grant funding, another by fee-for-service billing, and a third by capitated payments. Each focused on their part of the elephant; and as a result, each group had a different solution for how to solve the financial shortfall.

Grant Funding

Over the years, Community Connections has received grants for many things—serving homeless women, delivering testing and psychiatric support to women with HIV, and designing a treatment model for men and women suffering from the aftermath of abuse. Grants typically bring revenue into the organization for three to five years, but you can't count on them to make up for a revenue shortfall because the money can, and often does, go away.

When confronted with the revenue shortfall, the department heads who were supported by grant money had a targeted and somewhat simplistic perspective: solve the problem by getting more grants and focus on grants that had the highest dollar value. Unfortunately, this strategy had a few downsides. It took time and energy to find and apply for appropriate funding. Some of the grants incurred additional costs such as hiring a head researcher to evaluate outcomes and some of the opportunities stretched the limits of our competencies. Unfortunately, grants could contribute to a solution, but they were rarely big enough to solve more than a small portion of the problem.

Fee-for-Service Funding

Those who brought money into Community Connections by billing for every discrete service they provided had a very different perspective on the revenue shortfall problem. From their point of view, the solution was also very simple: bill more services. Even though this perspective was consistent with the strategy used by many legal, medical, and financial practitioners, it was not well aligned with the mission of the organization.

Most nonprofit organizations see themselves as driven by an altruistic cause. People in such organizations are motivated more by how much good they do than by how many services they bill. Yet increasing the number of services was a perspective that needed to be given extra weight. After all, since fee-for-service billing was the primary way in which Community Connections made its money, it was seen as the biggest part of the elephant. Increasing the units of service billed seemed like an obvious way to fix the revenue problem.

The first thing that needed to be done was to explain the rationale for this perspective to the staff who would need to increase their billable services. Because so many staff were trained to work in human services and not in finance, it wasn't easy for them to understand the connection between the work they did and the money it generated. Most felt that if they worked hard, they were doing their share to keep the organization solvent. When only billable hours were considered to be "productive hours," many young staff began to believe that the organization didn't value all of the extra services they provided—services that were not paid for by insurance companies.

All frontline clinicians were asked to generate five hours of billable service per day. Some staff worked extra hard in order to make sure that they did not fall short of the needed number of hours, while others grumbled that the work was just too hard and began to look elsewhere for another job. In either case, employees reported that "stress over productivity" was the number one cause for dissatisfaction with the job.

Still seeing the revenue problem through the fee-for-service lens, senior management came up with several methods by which productivity numbers could be increased: rewarding highly productive staff, providing extra training for all staff on how to do their work more effectively and efficiently, warning underperformers, and then, if necessary, terminating staff who could not meet productivity standards.

Capitated Funding

In a capitated system, providers get paid for the number of people they see, not for the number of services they provide. The organization gets paid the capitated rate even if the client is only seen once a month. For those who look at the revenue problem from the perspective of per person payments, the answer to increasing revenues is again quite simple: see more clients.

Community Connections received a precalculated reimbursement rate per client (much like a managed care organization) and was then responsible for providing all necessary behavioral health care services (except those delivered at a hospital). Thus, there was a financial incentive to provide enough service, but not to provide too much service. Because of savings from economies of scale, it was to our advantage to take as many clients as we could manage. Caseloads went up considerably without a corresponding increase in administrative overhead.

This seemed positive on the surface but posed a dilemma for clinical service providers. The insurance provider paid equally for a client whether he or she was seen as little as once a month or as much as five times a week. The rate did not increase because of more service. The incentive was to limit service while increasing head count. Some staff questioned whether this model actually had the effect of compromising care and they protested that it gave them the feeling that they were working in a "Medicaid mill."

A capitated system works best when at least some of the clients in the pool really need only minimal service, but Community Connections generally serves people who are heavy users of care. Low users go elsewhere. Our youngest clinicians in particular—those who were the most idealistic and committed to the work—resented having to monitor, and probably limit, the amount of care they delivered. Of all the payment systems, we found that this one required the greatest shift in perspective by supervisors and managers. Big caseloads and limited service seemed antithetical to the role of caregiver. It required a major change in perspective to help senior practitioners understand that good care might actually mean less care.

Each of the three parts of the elephant (and in the end there were more than three) represented a different perspective on how to understand and address the problem of a revenue shortfall. Some departments advocated for spending resources on getting more grants, others argued for finding ways to generate more services, and still others wanted to expand the client base. In the end, the CEO and the CFO had to decide how energy and resources should been spent, but this left some employees feeling ignored and ultimately less invested in solving the problem. Multiple perspectives can add new ideas and energies to solving problems, but when there are limited resources, multiple perspectives can pose a barrier to actually getting the problem resolved.

CASE STUDY #3: NOT REALLY WANTING TO SOLVE THE PROBLEM

As strange as it may seem, there are some problems that we really don't want to solve. Some of the reasons are obvious and others are much more obscure. To start, fixing a problem often means disrupting a process that has been in place for a very long time or it may cause interpersonal headaches that become problematic in themselves. Some problems may remain unsolved because they disrupt the underground life of the organization.

Case managers at Community Connections often have to drive several miles a day in order to see clients who live in different parts of the city. The problem of how to reimburse staff members for their mileage expenses became increasingly complicated as the organization grew. At first, the method was rather simple. A case manager would tell his supervisor how far he had driven and receive reimbursement, often without mileage receipts and often from petty cash. Obviously this method was sloppy, subject to fraud, and impossible to track at the time of an audit.

A new method was devised by the accounting department that involved filling out a paper form, attaching actual receipts, getting the approval of a supervisor, and then receiving a check at the end of the month. Once again, this method eventually became more and more difficult to maintain. Receipts were lost, time required by accounting staff to administer the program grew, and delays in processing the reimbursement meant that some people had to wait for several payroll cycles before they received their reimbursement. It would seem obvious that this process needed to be streamlined and changed. But even after we purchased new software that would automate the process, staff resisted change. They complained about the old way, but no one really wanted to change it. People feared that the new method would end up being slower, accounting staff did not want to give up their role/power in controlling reimbursements, and supervisory staff wanted to be able to use the mileage reimbursement system to track just where their employees were going.

Despite the years of complaints about the system, no one seemed eager to cooperate in changing the system they "hated." Better the devil you know than the one you don't. After almost three years, the new process was put in place and management took away the pens and paper and required that everyone switch over to the new system. And of course everyone asked why we had not done this sooner!

Some problems don't get solved, not because of process but because of people. In a number of instances, team leaders worry that solving a problem will hurt someone's feelings. In a larger, more impersonal business this may sound silly, but in a founder-run business where many folks have worked there for a long time it factors into solving problems. In the early 1990s, after almost ten years of rapid growth, Community Connections needed to make some hard choices about where to put its energies. In other words, which departments should get support and which should be allowed to wind down?

There were several times over the years when Community Connections had to face the problem of how to manage a dysfunctional department. In some cases, the department was in financial trouble, other cases involved a department that had too many employees, but in most instances the department was not performing its intended functions. In each case, the organization had to face the human cost of solving the problem. People were dependent on having a paycheck, or they had a child to take care of, or they were facing a serious illness. Solving organizational problems would mean that individual employees would experience personal problems, so management avoided taking action. Problems with interpersonal consequences were problems the organization did not want to solve.

Finally, there are problems that organizations do not want to resolve for reasons that are less immediately apparent. Most departments in an organization perform the functions they are designated and designed to perform. The IT department is the IT department and it provides IT services. But that is not always the case. In the covert life of an organization, there are some departments that perform a function other than the one for which they were designed.

At Community Connections, the HR department served the function of being the organization's all-purpose scapegoat. Most times, when there was a problem, whether it had to do with finances or quality improvement or some other management issue, someone in the leadership group would comment, "Well, you know that's HR's fault." Now it was true that the HR department did have problems: it was understaffed and had a poorly defined mission, but it was *not* responsible for most of the problems the organization experienced. Many knew that if the problems with HR were fixed, there would be no one to blame when things went wrong. Other people would have to look at their departments and figure out how they contributed to organizational problems. It was much easier to keep HR in its place and use the all-purpose explanation, "The dog ate my homework."

In some ways this section has been counterintuitive. On the surface it seems reasonable and logical that people who run businesses should want to solve problems that get in the way of reaching goals. But as we all know, that isn't always the case. And issues of precedent, interpersonal strife, and covert missions all pose barriers to really getting problems solved.

CASE STUDY #4: BEING AFRAID OF MAKING A MISTAKE

Mistakes are all around us. Little ones like forgetting to bring an umbrella on a rainy day; big ones like accepting the wrong job; and catastrophic ones like failing to douse a fire in a dry forest. Regardless of the magnitude, it is impossible to avoid making mistakes. Yet many nonprofit organizations are so risk averse that they seem frozen in place.

Sometimes the fear of making a mistake is in direct proportion to the cost of getting it wrong, but other times, often reflecting the fears of leaders, mistakes are to be avoided even if the downside is relatively minor. Yet in start-up nonprofits, growth only comes from the willingness to innovate, to try new things, and perhaps to throw caution to the wind. But first, what are some of the mistakes that businesses might be extra cautious about making?

Financial Mistakes

The impact of making a financial mistake can be far-reaching for an organization that starts with a very small budget. It goes without saying that an organization must pay its employees. But what about pay increases? Giving too high of an increase might turn into a big financial mistake, but giving little or no increase might result in good people leaving the organization.

Another financial concern involves the acquisition and distribution of resources. Because Community Connections has always been in a phase of expansion, the question of office space is one that arises frequently. The problem to be solved concerns how many resources should we put into acquiring new space. Should we buy space, rent it, increase the number of square feet we need? While we are waiting to make a decision, do we squeeze people into a small space or do we delay starting a new program? For an organization committed to service delivery, advocacy, or community development, decisions about space may seem overly bureaucratic, but they are essential to getting the work done. A wise mentor once said to me, "When space opens up, see it, grab it, and don't let it go."

Legal Mistakes

A young organization cannot afford to be sued. Lawsuits cost money, absorb time, and diminish morale. When you are afraid of being sued, you are not free to make needed clinical, personnel, and strategic decisions. All of a sudden "what's good for the business" gets replaced by "what's going to get us in trouble."

Especially at the beginning of an organization's life, before policies and procedures have been put in place, the possibility of making mistakes can be great. The fear of committing an error, however, goes against the entrepreneurial spirit that inspired the organization to begin with. Balancing risk taking with caution can be a good formula for creating a steady, careful business. It is probably not the hallmark of a very innovative one.

Political Mistakes

Political mistakes are not necessarily relevant to all organizations. These are the mistakes that involve dealing with an outside regulatory board— often a board whose approval or disapproval can determine the success and even the viability of the company. Consider medical device start-ups that may need FDA approval, or health clinics that might require certification and licensure, or technology ventures that will need to secure outside capital.

Community Connections has frequently had to respond to outside licensing boards and insurance vendors. There is often a concern that if these relationships are not managed well that there will be serious consequences. At one point, the organization had to negotiate with a vendor about a payment schedule for money owed to us. We were so concerned that if we made a mistake our payments would be delayed, or worse still, denied, that it took us over a month to write a simple e-mail laying out our case for payment.

It is often difficult for start-ups, who see themselves as nimble, innovative ventures, to acknowledge that fear may play a part in the difficulty they have solving problems.

CASE STUDY #5: LACKING THE NECESSARY SKILLS

It seems obvious that any business, whether a start-up or a more established organization, should not take on projects for which it does not have the necessary skills. So why then does this happen all the time? At the beginning, new companies are eager for business and so they take on projects for which they are only minimally qualified.

New organizations want the business. Several years ago, a senior manager at Community Connections was notified that a large grant to deliver addictions services was being posted. No staff had any expertise in this area, but we thought, "How hard can it be, after all, we provide mental health services to hundreds of clients?" What we learned after we were awarded the grant was that treating people with mental illness was very different from treating people with severe addictions. Not only were we lacking the professional skills, but we also did not have the security and the medical resources that were necessary. We were so eager for new business, a situation very common for young start-ups, that we failed to ask if we actually had the needed skills to take on the project.

In some cases, the lack of skills is easy to admit. The missing skills are in an area far afield from the organization's core business. Take for example, a social service business that has to manage IT support. Staff members might complain, somewhat naively, that "the computers are not working." But that is as far as they can go. They don't know what they don't know; somewhat like taking a car to the dealership because it is making a funny noise. Once you get to the station your ability to describe the problem ceases.

With a poorly functioning IT system, Community Connections was forced to get outside help to solve the problem. But once again ignorance got in the way. If you can't really understand a problem, how do you know if an outside operator can solve it? That's where getting a second opinion makes sense.

Bringing in outside expertise, however, is much more difficult when the missing skills involve an organization's or a department's core business. For years, Community Connections struggled with how to manage the accounting department. The leaders within the department were all certified accountants, so every time a problem was identified the in-house staff asserted that they could fix it. Asking for help when you are "supposed" to have the needed skills requires a level of self-awareness that is often difficult to achieve.

And finally, organizations lack the skills to perform well because they just don't have the right staff. There is often an inclination, especially in "do-good" nonprofits, to try to make it work with every employee. But at the end of the day, organizations need to have employees with the right skills to do the job and that might just mean having to let someone go.

Solving problems is challenging enough, but we always make it more difficult by getting in our own way. Certainly we can't solve a problem we don't see or don't understand, but we also can't solve problems when our own fear or uncertainty or lack of motivation gets in the way. It would be nice to believe that there are problems we can solve without having to contend with barriers big and small, but in truth, barriers go with problem solving as a natural part of things.

A PERSONAL NOTE FROM MAXINE

It has always been the case that once I think I have figured out how to solve a problem, I move quickly to action. Sometimes, I may spend more time arguing with myself (or more than likely, with others) about my solution, but often I am willing to accept the consequences of moving fast rather than slowing the pace down.

There were many times over the years when Community Connections was presented with a problem that needed solving. Sometimes when I was meeting with a group of people, someone would challenge my reasoning and say, "We can't do that." If I was alone or with just one person and needed to make a decision, I would go with my gut and make the decision that seemed right. My partner Helen would frequently take me aside and asked me what I had come up with. It's not that she thought I was wrong, but rather, as she often said, "I want to know what you promised, just in case someone asks me!" My mantra had become, "Say you are going to fix the problem first and then figure out if you can make it happen."

There were clearly times when I made mistakes and needed to come up with new solutions to the same problem. My style was "See it, say it, do it." Some of my solutions worked because I was so certain that they would. And I wasn't faking it; once I thought I had the right answer, I moved ahead quickly. My husband has said about me, jokingly (I think), "sometimes wrong, but never in doubt."

PUTTING PROBLEM SOLVING AT COMMUNITY CONNECTIONS IN CONTEXT

Collaborative problem solving is one of the most critical skills in contemporary workplaces. Why? Largely because there are fewer and fewer routine, individual tasks. Repetition, rote, and routine have given way to more sophisticated, interactive tasks. With technological change continuing its steady march, and robots further infiltrating many aspects of our lives, the need for individuals, teams, and organizations to solve complex problems has grown dramatically.

As the preceding section indicated, Community Connections is no exception. There has been a steady (but unpredictable) diet of significant changes in insurance and other funding streams, federal and local regulations, and the nature of trauma and its treatments. These changes have required Community Connections to overcome barriers of understanding, framing, diagnosis, prioritization, will, and skill. In this chapter's final section, we reflect on those barriers and what social science has to say about hurdling them.

In today's increasingly diverse workplace, especially in cities like Washington, D.C., where Community Connections operates, solving problems requires collaboration across age, gender, ethnicity, as well as educational, functional, occupational, and other boundaries. While potentially advantageous for solving complex problems, this diversity is also a potential liability. People with different backgrounds can "see" or frame the same problem differently, and have divergent views about how to solve it.

Changes in how organizations think about hiring and training have the potential to improve problem solving by changing the skill sets of new employees. For example, individuals with a higher tolerance for ambiguity are likely to be more successful solving problems in nonroutine environments. Individuals who are agile learners (and have varied backgrounds) are also likely to be more effective in workplaces where problem solving is a necessity.[4] However, hiring those likely to be better problem solvers is difficult and must be paired with process-based approaches to tackle problems more effectively.

Traditional approaches to problem solving include Six Sigma and quality management. They tend to be quite linear and data driven. More recently, as discussed in chapter 2, design thinking has emerged as an approach to both creative and problem-solving tasks. It is still fundamentally data driven (with empathy and user-driven stories among the most important types of data), but it also involves a different approach to problem solving—an approach rooted in careful framing and reframing before rushing to solutions.

Pushing people and teams to think about how they're framing problems, and then support them through various rounds of reframing is one of the most important ways to improve problem solving. For example, the property manager for a high-rise office building was besieged by complaints about how slow the elevators were. The manager engaged three consultants to develop solutions that would speed up the elevators. The cost would be high, but they told him they could cut wait times in half with some changes to the elevators' computer operating system. The day before he was poised to sign a million-dollar contract to fix the elevators, the property manager was sitting in a barbershop waiting for a haircut. He was surrounded by mirrors and watching a football game on wall-mounted TVs over the barbers' chairs. After fifteen minutes, he realized he hadn't balked at the delay and asked himself, "Why am I about to spend a million dollars to shorten a sixty-second wait?" The next morning, he assembled his team and suggested they reframe the elevator wait time problem as a boredom and predictability problem. Once they did, and once he told his barbershop story, they stood the problem on its head.

How could they make the elevators' arrival more predictable and how could they make the wait less boring? For less than one-tenth of the planned computer fix, they installed mirrors on the doors of the elevators (figuring that people would welcome the opportunity to check their clothes and hair before heading up to the office). They also hung flat-panel TVs between the elevators so that people could watch the morning *Market Watch* and celebrity gossip shows depending on where they stood. Finally, they realized that the manager's fifteen-minute barbershop wait was tolerable for patrons partly because they could see who was in front of them in line (and make continuously updated mental estimates of how long before it would be their turn in the chair). In response, they replaced the simple LED display telling you what floor the elevator was on, with a countdown timer showing people how long before the elevator arrived. Once they reframed the problem from wait times to boredom and predictability, they unlocked a whole range of low-cost solutions that dramatically reduced complaints about slow elevators.

More frames, different frames, frames based on metaphors for the underlying problem, and analogical thinking can all help push teams before they even get to the point of solving the problem. In the elevator example, the rush to solution development nearly cost them hundreds of thousands of dollars. A late-breaking reminder to be sure they were solving the right problem ended up saving money and improving satisfaction.

SUGGESTED READINGS

For more on problem solving, see the chapter titled "Nudge, Test, and Escalate Gradually: Problem-Solving Strategies for Quiet Leaders" in Joe Badaracco, *Leading Quietly* (Boston, MA: Harvard Business School Press, 2008); Sara L. Beckman and Michael Barry, "Framing and Re-Framing: Core Skills for a Complex World," *Harvard Business Review,*

January 1, 2015; and Dwayne Spradlin, "Are You Solving the Right Problem?" *Harvard Business Review*, September 2012. Michael Kallet's *Think Smarter: Critical Thinking to Improve Problem-Solving and Decision-Making Skills* (New York: Wiley, 2014) is also a good starting point.

The type of problem you're facing should also guide your reading. For example, many problems are fundamentally about decision making or creativity, in which case books on those topics would be especially helpful (if not framed specifically as books about problem solving). For example, see Leigh Thompson's excellent *Creative Conspiracy: The New Rules of Breakthrough Collaboration* (Boston, MA: Harvard Business School Press, 2013) or Chip and Dan Heath's *Decisive: How to Make Better Choices in Life and Work* (New York: Crown, 2013).

6

ENGAGING THE OUTSIDE WORLD

Is Anyone Out There?

Just like a butterfly develops in a cocoon, most founder-run organizations begin in a safe, small space. One person, maybe a few friends or colleagues, start talking and thinking and expanding on an idea. Maybe they reach a point where they want to bring others in to help take the idea to the next stage. Eventually their world starts to expand. Others, however, keep their private space private for a very long time, believing that their best thinking takes place inside, not outside, the box.

At some point, however, even the most insular organizations need to turn their attention outward, toward the community and the context in which it does business. Who are its potential partners and possible allies? Where is the competition coming from? What changes in the external environment will have the greatest impact? For an organization that has survived and even thrived in isolation, this turning outward can bring struggles, conflict, but best of all, it can lead to unexpected opportunities. Remember, butterflies that stay in the cocoon eventually wither and die. The following fable tells the tale of three brothers with dramatically different approaches to dealing with the world beyond their own small, narrow spaces.

A FABLE: THE THREE BROTHERS

Once there were three brothers who lived side by side in identical cabins in the center of town. Early each morning, they would step outside of their cabins and greet one another with a hearty hello. After doing a few chores, each would retreat into the comfort of his own cabin, only to emerge again the next morning when the sun rose.

But something different would happen to each of the brothers once they were inside their cabins. The first brother would walk to the big window at the front of the cabin and pull the shutters closed. He would then place the big iron latch across the shutters so that no light could come in. "How safe I am inside my cabin," he would say to himself, "no one can see in and I don't have to be bothered by all the noise outside." Then he would sit down in his favorite chair, light a candle, and proceed to read until it was time to go to sleep and wait for morning to come.

The second brother would also walk to the big window at the front of his cabin, but he would only pull the curtain closed. He would leave the big shutters open so that light could enter the cabin, and every once and a while he would walk to the window and open the curtains just enough so that he could peer outside. He always made sure, however, that he hunched down low so that no one could see him looking out.

Finally, the third brother would also walk to the big window at the front of his cabin, but he would fling the shutters wide open and pull the curtain back and sit in front of the window all day. He would wave to his neighbors and watch all the activity going on outside in the street. He kept his window open and sometimes a neighbor would walk up to the window and offer him some vegetables from the garden, tell him the latest piece of gossip, or just stop so they could enjoy the fresh air together. And sometimes the third brother would walk outside his front door and wander to the end of the street. It was not long, however, before he returned to the comfort of his cottage; but now, he would sit by his window and think about what he had seen.

Occasionally when the brothers met in the morning they would argue over who had found the best way to treat the world outside of his cabin, but in the end, each would go back inside, feeling quite satisfied with how he had chosen to live.

That is not quite the whole story, however; once there were actually four brothers, but when the fourth brother went inside his cabin, he had a habit of throwing the shutters open and pulling the curtains back as far as he could and flinging his door wide open. He would keep the door open for many days on end. And he lived like that for several days at a time, until one day when a gang of thieves stormed into his cabin and tore it all to shreds.

Organizations, new businesses, and established founder-run organizations all exist in a social/professional context. While they may start in a creative cocoon, incubating and growing, gaining their nourishment from the inside, eventually they need to emerge into the more complex world outside.

So how do you decide how much to engage with the world outside your own organization? In the fairy tale of "The Three Brothers," the first brother stays in a safe but limited world. He would have no idea if a ferocious tornado were barreling down on the village. The second brother would know enough to be prepared for a disaster, but certainly not enough to take advantage of a new opportunity. But the third brother would experience enough contact to know what was going on in the world outside his cottage, engage in enough friendly discourse so that he made as few enemies as possible, and gather enough information so that he could sit and think and decide on the right strategy to bring him the greatest benefit. He could also hear the latest gossip so that he would know when a new opportunity was about to present itself. The fourth brother, because he let himself be seduced by the outside world, could not see danger and was ultimately destroyed.

If Community Connections had followed the strategy of the fourth brother, the story would end right here. But throughout its history, Community Connections dealt with the outside world like one of the first three brothers: either too little contact, too much engagement, or contact that feels just right.

CASE STUDY #1: TOO LITTLE ENGAGEMENT

At the very beginning of its development, Community Connections's founders made the conscious decision to fly below the radar screen. What this meant practically was that the organization would keep its plans and its activities out of the public spotlight. While this may sound a bit paranoid, and part of it certainly was, it grew out of a careful read of the business landscape and an assessment of the founders' combined skills.

In 1984, the idea of downsizing large residential mental health institutions and finding ways for patients to live successfully in community settings was already part of the conversation about how to provide humane and affordable care. But in Washington, D.C., despite a lawsuit filed in 1975 and an optimistic start, a major effort to empty St. Elizabeths hospital had not yet begun.[1] Community Connections was funded as somewhat of a pilot program to see if community treatment was in fact doable. As a result, some of the strategies employed by Community Connections were untested (as is the case with many companies trying out new models), and while supporters wanted to see successful outcomes, there were others who had tangible resources to lose if community treatment was to go forward on a large scale. Community Connections's founders decided to keep their heads down, work hard, and wait for the results to come in.

Like the first brother in the fairy tale, the founders closed the shutters to the cabin and instead of thinking that there is "no such thing as bad publicity,"[2] the founders feared that at this early stage in the development of Community Connections any speculation of failure might mean trouble. This began a pattern of acting like a phantom company as far as the media was concerned. The founders refused to be part of news stories about the progress of deinstitutionalization and on the few occasions when they did talk to a local reporter, they gave vague answers or hid behind the veil of client confidentiality. Internally there were discussions about how to handle the press and efforts were made to direct all conversations with the broader community to one of the cofounders. Managing the outside world kept Community Connections safe, but it also cost opportunities.

In addition to its low media profile, Community Connections's founders avoided city politics. The city council had several hearings that raised issues regarding mental health policy, and Community Connections was often not at the table. Giving the rationale that the meetings were often unproductive, the founders failed to make contacts that might have been useful when they wanted to advocate for particular positions. It should be noted that this avoidance of becoming involved in the outside world was born not only out of caution, but also of naiveté, competitiveness, and arrogance.

Having no background in business, the founders did not recognize a big part of how business gets done. They believed that if they just did their jobs, and did them well, then political and local connections would be irrelevant. Not realizing that relationships are a critical part of collaboration and negotiating and compromise—all necessary for a business to survive—the founders failed to make important connections.

Competitiveness also contributed to the decision to keep a low profile. Like the second brother, Community Connections's leadership occasionally peeked through the curtains, but did not go much further. Staff were jokingly cautioned, "If you go to a meeting, listen a lot, steal what you can, and give away nothing." As city resources shrank and more organizations with the same mission came on the scene, it seemed more and more important to keep quiet about plans and strategies. At one point, one of the cofounders got involved in a local advocacy group, but when she did, it was not to participate as a coequal member, but rather to take control of the group. In that way she could be part of the outside world but do it on her own terms.

Finally, leadership at Community Connections stayed away from the outside world out of a sense of arrogance. Believing that they could do the job better than anyone else, they minimized what they could learn from others. This arrogance resulted in others saying or thinking, "Just because they are big, they think they are better than everyone else." This reputation occasionally deprived Community Connections from obtaining new opportunities, and it also led to other organizations just waiting for Community Connections to take a fall.

Despite some early indications that the strategy of flying low was having negative consequences, Community Connections's leadership continued to believe that low visibility was an advantage. That belief manifested itself in three other ways: the selection of a board of directors, decisions about fundraising, and the use of social media.

Like many founder-run organizations, Community Connections began with a friendly, small, and family-dominated board of directors. Most of the power was vested in the two founders and their spouses. Additional members joined the board over the years, most serving for long periods of time. Members were chosen for their trust, their friendship, and their loyalty to Community Connections. Rarely were members chosen for the expertise they might bring to the board (but luckily all of them brought talents and opinions that were helpful in moving the organization forward). In those early years, before the death of one of the cofounders, what was most important was that board members would give the founders free rein to do as they chose.

Board members were never asked to be involved in fundraising or other tangibly supportive activities since the founders considered their participation on the board primarily an act of friendship. The failure to be involved in fundraising went beyond the board, however. Fundraising would mean becoming a more public business. Community Connections was the equivalent of a privately held company. We issued yearly financial statements as was required, but we continued to keep our shutters tightly closed. Other organizations spent time planning fundraising galas, and while these events netted very little income, what they did do was raise an organization's profile. For some organizations, one thing led to another and fundraising turned into more publicity, which turned into more grants, which then led to more income to start new projects. At one point, Community Connections borrowed the philosophy of the investment firm Smith Barney, "They make money the old-fashioned way. They earn it."[3]

After several years of remaining insulated and isolated behind the curtains, Community Connections began to see the downside of hiding safely in its own little cottage. In addition to the missed opportunities already mentioned, we failed to see the growth of a whole new way of communicating—the power of social media. Community Connections had built a rudimentary website (initially without any outside professional help) and it read like a page out of an academic journal. The website was rarely accessed, provided little important information, failed to highlight some of Community Connections's accomplishments, and told the world that we had not kept up with the changing ways of communicating. It was not until the communications mantle was passed to a younger generation of leaders that we began to use media to open our doors, but in a way where we had much more control than we ever imagined. Although there are reasons for keeping the contact with the outside world small in the early stages of organizational growth, it becomes less and less wise as the organization progresses.

CASE STUDY #2: TOO MUCH ENGAGEMENT

As is so often the case with engagement, the pendulum can swing too far. As both Community Connections and the care system grew, it became increasingly difficult to stay in our own little world. We made a conscious decision to engage with city planners, other agencies occupying our same business space, community leaders, and local politicians. But because we had little experience engaging with our community, we found ourselves to be novices in the world of networking. And like most novices, we had a steep learning curve and we made mistakes.

It might sound a little extreme to say that the cofounders were naive since they obviously had experience negotiating and reading the risks and opportunities of the business environment, but they had often done so at a distance. Opening the door to the outside world means getting your hands dirty.

Several members of Community Connections staff began going to city planning meetings and contributing their ideas to the city's strategic plan for delivering mental health services. But since several staff members were going to a variety of meetings and we had no centralized way for sharing information internally, we often found ourselves needing an interpreter to manage the flow of information. We went from closing the shutters to flinging the door wide open when it might have been wise to spend just a little time peering around the curtains.

One consequence of being out there was that no one internally or externally knew who spoke for Community Connections. Staff wondered if they were just connecting to other agencies in order to listen and learn, or did they have the authority to establish strategic partnerships. As an organization, we kept asking ourselves, "Why are we out there anyway?" And networking takes time. At one point we conducted a survey designed to assess the satisfaction of line staff and one of the big complaints was that supervisors were so busy going to meetings that they had no time to do their "real" jobs. Engaging with the outside community is somewhat like taking a trip. You don't have to plan every moment of the vacation, but it does help to have a destination.

Since Community Connections was the biggest nonprofit behavioral health organization in the city and had been in operation longer than most others, it was naturally the case that Community Connections staff knew people across other organizations. In fact, many Community Connections staff transferred to other similar organizations over the years. Many management staff found themselves wondering, "What is the difference between building relationships, forging collaborations, and gossiping or sharing internal plans that might compromise Community Connections's competitive advantage?" Individuals and the organization as a whole needed to learn the differences and to understand that growing networks is fundamentally about building relationships.

Perhaps the biggest mistake that Community Connections made when it opened its doors wide was giving away valuable intellectual property. For years, staff at Community Connections had worked to develop a model for delivering services to individuals who had suffered abuse in childhood or adulthood. The model was refined, piloted, and used with several hundred clients. It had also been turned into a formal manual for use by a wide range of providers, tested for reliability and fidelity, and then judged to be an evidence-based practice (giving it high status in a health care world increasingly valuing outcomes and model fidelity). The principles of the trauma approach were then scaled up to apply to whole systems of care.

The model, known as Trauma Recovery and Empowerment, received federal and local accolades.[4] Then the designers made a big decision. They decided to open source the model. Their decision would give universal, free access to the product. This was certainly a generous act and was founded on the belief that "if we have something good and it has the potential of helping a large number of people, why not share it?" We were not asking people to help us design the product; we were merely making an already developed product available.

But there were a number of unanticipated consequences. First, people did not use the model as it had been designed, tested, and validated. Individual providers made their own alterations so that after a while, the model as it was being implemented was a poorly rendered copy of the original. Once you fling the door open, you have no real control over who comes in.

Second, there was a less noble consequence: the designers of the model wanted credit or acknowledgment for what they had created. Initially, public credit came in abundance, but over time, the industry seemed to forget just whose model this was anyway. Other programs, especially those that had made modifications in the model, began presenting it at conferences and industry meetings. A few began charging to consult to smaller organizations on how to implement the model and the funding sources began mandating that the systemwide version of the model be included in all behavioral health applications for funding.

Wow! People like our ideas, but wait a minute, what about us? In response, Community Connections began a nationwide training program and began charging mental health systems for providing protocols on how to implement the model. Trainers at Community Connections developed their own modification of the model, which they put into a separate manual and marketed to interested providers. To some extent, we were trying to put the toothpaste back in the tube. Leadership knew that they had to let the outside world in. They needed to share information, to learn what others were doing, and to build coalitions. But unlike the fourth brother in the fairy tale, they needed to approach the outside in a far more intentional way.

CASE STUDY # 3: CONTACT THAT FEELS JUST RIGHT

In their book *Great by Choice*, Jim Collins and Morton T. Hansen talk about charting a steady course of growth—not slowing down in good times or speeding up in bad times, but maintaining the same consistent pace.[5] That paradigm can be applied equally to an organization's relationship to the outside world—a constant state of engagement. Over the years, we have found a number of ways of getting it just right.

A good connection with the world outside of Community Connections meant developing good relationships. Connection is not like reading the newspaper and learning what's going on out there. It is fundamentally about building relationships, and relationships take time.

At the beginning of our growth, we waited until we needed something before we engaged with those beyond our doors. For example, we only met with the area neighborhood council when we wanted to address a complaint about one of our clients, or we needed a permit to hold an event on city property. Not surprisingly, since we were unknown to those in the neighborhood, our interactions were stilted, anonymous, and at times, downright hostile.

Over the years, we began to let ourselves become part of the community before we needed something. We cultivated relationships that were friendly and collaborative. People came to know us, what we did, why we did it, and on a personal level, who we were. When we had events for National Recovery Month in the park across from our offices, not only were neighbors agreeable, but they actively participated in making the event a success.[6]

Networking was no longer seen as a chore or a necessary evil. Moving beyond our obvious narrow business interests allowed us to invite collaboration and be included in new opportunities. One community member introduced us to local developers who were looking for partners to help manage difficult tenants living in their buildings. A new partnership grew from that contact.

Dealing with the world outside means both going out and letting others in. But this back and forth traffic is not the equivalent of a reconnaissance mission. It entails more than learning information; it involves building partnerships and sharing information and being willing to take the next step toward a legitimate collaboration. We have all heard the saying, "two heads are better than one." Well, sometimes two sets of ideas, two differing perspectives, or two sets of experiences are better than one.

More than just building relationships with outside players, Community Connections began acknowledging outside partners for the contributions they made in helping Community Connections become a better organization. Postings on social media thanked and acknowledged those outside the organization who had done something special to help consumers, to enhance the organization's mission, or to share new technologies. This was a very tangible way of demonstrating that in the course of doing business, the door swings both ways, and that we care about our partners not just as sources of information but as people we can trust.

In 2016, as part of a branding campaign, Community Connections came up with the phrase "Sharing Caring." We are an organization that cares about others and we wanted to share our caring spirit with others in our community. But then a young staff member pointed out that the phrase could just as well read in the other direction, "Caring Sharing," because we genuinely care about our partners who work with us to bring services to an impoverished community. Caring about others leads to sharing with one another. We don't just exchange information with the outside world, but we also build relationships.

For those who were a bit reserved about reaching out, we began to embrace some of the technology that allows an organization to engage with the outside world. Webinars and other computer-based learning opportunities allow an organization to open the door, engage with others, but to do so in the comfort of their own offices. It is possible to have as much interaction as you want or need and no more. Like one of the brothers in the fairy tale, organizations can have a peek outside the window, draw the curtains back, and then pull them shut again.

When applying for grants and outside funding, technology opened us up to long distance conversations with other organizations that shared our interests. All participants got to ask questions and hear the same answers. Even though grantees from different cities may never meet, they feel as if they know one another. In the early 1990s, Community Connections went through such a process when applying for a large federal grant. Long after the grant was over, staff members from one organization felt as if they knew and could share information with people from across the country. They were invited into one another's worlds without ever having shaken hands.

As part of getting our relationship with the outside world right, leaders at Community Connections began sharing the responsibility of making connections. When Community Connections was in its early years, there were only a few people and many jobs that needed attention. One staff member was assigned the responsibility of making outside connections. Gloria, who enjoyed connecting with colleagues outside the organization, frequently spoke up at citywide meetings. She became known to policymakers, competitors, and local and federal grantors who came to believe that she spoke for the organization and they began to treat her as a private practitioner who worked for herself, not for Community Connections. When Gloria unexpectedly fell ill and was forced to retire, Community Connections's relationships with the outside world retired as well. The organization found itself having to start all over again.

As we started to think of ourselves as a team, we realized that engaging with the outside world was a team sport rather than a solo one. When opportunities arose to engage with outside groups or even competitor organizations, we involved more than one person. Internally this gave the message that we were all part of Community Connections, all working toward the same mission. But it also sent the message to outside groups that single individuals were not operating alone. Sending and exposing more than one person also let people know any network-

ing connections that were initiated were for the benefit of the organization, not for the benefit of the individual.

Early in our development, we found ourselves needing to negotiate a
new contract for an expansion of services that we were asked to provide.
We initially sent a single representative who conducted the negotiation
from start to finish. But on one occasion, this person was out sick and
was unable to go, so a second staff member took her place. When the
two compared notes, it was startling that each had heard different mes-
sages and each had interpreted what she heard differently. So we
changed our procedures and now no one goes to a negotiation alone.
Sending two people is almost like having a built-in fact checker. And, of
course, there is the additional benefit of having more than one person
who gets a chance to engage with the outside world.

When we felt at a loss as to how to take the first step in evaluating
and restructuring our organization, we began to hire consultants who
would serve as guides. These folks were professional networkers and
they introduced us to contacts and possibilities that we would never
have found on our own. Consultants have the potential of paving the
way into the outside world and they tend to have a much broader view
of what's out there beyond your universe.

We do have one word of warning about the world of consultants,
however. Over the years, Community Connections has engaged the
help of many outside consultants. In the early years, our request was
simply, "We are floundering; please help us get back on track." With
such a vague mandate, it is no wonder that the consultations failed. In
one instance we sought the help of an individual who was known as an
expert in helping small businesses develop strategic plans and form
healthy networks. When we first approached him, we had no idea what
a strategic plan was, much less why we needed one. We had several
sessions, focusing primarily, at his initiation, on race relations in our city
and why we needed a more diverse board of directors. Now, remember,
neither big city politics, issues of social justice, or board composition
had anything to do with the reason for engaging the consultation.

After completing the sessions that we had paid for in advance, we
bid our consultant good-bye. In the absence of a well-articulated agenda of our own, the consultant filled the time with his own particular
interests. In a quote often attributed to Mark Twain, but actually initially said by J. Vernon Magee, "An expert is just an ordinary fellow from

another town."[7] When you don't know what you want, the chances are all you'll get is an ordinary guy.

In selecting a consultant, you need to have a well-articulated problem or question you want help solving or answering. The goals and format of the consultation, as well as the process by which it will be carried out, both need to be clear. Once the consultation is completed, you don't have to accept all of the recommendations. After all, they are just recommendations.

At times, Community Connections leadership felt anxious about making a difficult decision. They felt concerned about the potential fallout from staff. One of our more savvy consultants suggested that we let him be the fall guy. If our recommendations were questioned, then all we had to do was say, "Well, the consultant said . . . ." In this way, we could present our decision without having to assume any responsibility!

Engaging a consultant does not necessarily mean that you are obliged to take her advice. Just because you let the salesman in the door doesn't mean that you have to buy the product. On the other hand, don't engage a consultant if you have no intention of listening to what they have to say. At one point, Community Connections was experimenting with implementing a new business model with a group of new partners. An expert in the field was engaged to help with the process, and within a few days she made some very cogent observations and gave some clear recommendations, recommendations that leadership proceeded to ignore. The organization had invested heavily in the new model and really just wanted someone to give it the seal of approval.

Expert consultants should be invited in for only a limited amount of time to advise on a specific problem. And while the analogy might be a bit overstated, Benjamin Franklin's famous statement, "Guests, like fish, begin to smell after three days" might just as easily be applied to consultants.[8]

Finally, we began to realize that venturing out of the world of Community Connections and the domain of mental health provided certain opportunities. We already knew many of the struggles and opportunities that our own world held, so we began to introduce ourselves to people in adjacent businesses: people who worked for the schools, the police department, and in parks and recreation, among others. We found, and continue to find, that new contacts lead to new relationships and potentially to new partnerships. We started to follow this piece of wisdom about innovation: "If you talk only to yourself, you stay the way you are. If you talk only to others in health care, you move with the pack. It's only if you talk with others outside of your domain that you can leap boundaries."[9]

No one doubts that it can be difficult to move beyond one's comfort zone and engage the outside, but it is possible and the benefits can be huge. The "us against the world" mentality has to be replaced with an "us with the world" vision. There is no choice if an organization is to grow and thrive. Almost four hundred years ago, in 1624, the poet John Donne wrote these famous lines, "No man is an island, entire of itself, every man is a piece of the continent, a part of the main."[10]

A PERSONAL NOTE FROM MAXINE

I have always thought of myself as a shy person, the kind who hangs back at parties, gets nervous giving public talks and meeting new people. In fact, I have successfully gone to parties, given talks, and met scores of new people. When I tell people I feel shy, they look at me as if I am putting them on, or as if I completely lack self-awareness. But what matters is how I feel, not, in this case, how others see me.

This self-perception has resulted in my being the inside person at Community Connections. It has always been someone else, at first my partner and then any one of a number of senior staff, who has gone out to engage the world. When some of our young staff would attend a local meeting or negotiate a new relationship with an outside vendor, I would always send them off with a caution, "Learn what you can, give away nothing, and do as much snooping while still being polite." This was a somewhat paranoid message, rendered by someone who saw herself as too shy or reluctant to do the engaging herself.

The more I nurtured my invisible persona, the less people came to expect that they would see me at professional gatherings. On one occasion, a city spokesperson turned to my partner and said half-jokingly, "I bet Maxine doesn't even exist. You just invented her so you'll have some cover if things go wrong!"

PUTTING ENGAGING THE OUTSIDE WORLD AT COMMUNITY CONNECTIONS IN CONTEXT

As "The Three Brothers" fable and case studies in this chapter highlight, it doesn't always come naturally for organizations to look beyond their own windows and doors. Sometimes we deliberately remain inwardly oriented—because of concerns about sharing critical information and worries about competitors taking advantage of any openings in our armor. Sometimes we do it unintentionally—just because we get so heads down and busy that we forget to engage with the outside world as often as we should. This heads-down busyness is especially common for new ventures when the founding team members are scrambling to get and keep their endeavor running. Before long, it can become habitual. In this commentary section, we describe how such behavior is typical, how it's grounded in a well-known (and evolutionarily rational) sequence of behaviors called the threat-rigidity effect, and how organizations can strike the right balance in terms of engaging with key stakeholders outside their doors.

At all levels of life—organism, individual, group, and organization—scholars Barry Staw, Lloyd Sandelands, and Jane Dutton have shown that perceived threats trigger a very predictable response.[11] At the organism level, threats trigger a flight, flee, or freeze response. At the individual, team, or organizational level, when we feel threatened, we restrict the flow of information, tighten controls, and revert to our comfort zones. We become less adaptive, more rigid in our thoughts and behaviors, and often add more rules and regulations. This generally involves focusing on the thing that the individual, team, or organization does best—its core product or service—and not doing other things including engaging with the external environment.

Based on complementary research by team scholars Deborah Ancona and Henrik Bresman, as well as Connie Gersick and Richard Hackman, we know that project teams tend to be extremely inwardly oriented for at least half of their life cycles. Left to its own devices, the average team won't look outside its own team boundaries until it gets halfway to its deadline. We also know that this internal orientation can be extremely counterproductive for teams. When teams are explicit about having members play externally oriented roles, they tend to perform better.

As Ancona, Bresman, and Katrin Käufer have noted, "The current environment demands a new brand of team—one that emphasizes outreach to stakeholders and adapts easily to flatter organizational structures, changing information and increasing complexity."[12] They have identified four key externally oriented roles, including scouts, guards, ambassadors, and coordinators. It is easy to think of comparable behaviors at the individual level or comparable roles at the organizational level (performed by one or more people).

As their name suggests, *scouts* gather information about what lies ahead and around—both within the organization and in the environment more broadly. They help find relevant knowledge and expertise. They also assess markets, technologies, and service delivery modes/models. In addition, they keep an eye out for potential partners and competitors (recognizing that a competitor might become a partner or vice versa). When the environment is especially volatile and competitive, scouts must remain particularly vigilant—always scanning beyond their boundaries. This scouting activity helps ensure that an outside view becomes part of forecasting and strategic decision-making processes, which Nobel prize–winner Daniel Kahneman notes can often be led astray by a tendency for an inwardly focused orientation.[13]

Community Connections had a general sense of its environment, but it didn't actively scout (or assign people to do so) until later in its life. As noted earlier, this insularity is common but can also be costly. Competitors can emerge unseen. Potential partnerships can be overlooked. Insularity is often the result of concerns about sharing intellectual property. This was true for Community Connections after its treatment model was adopted and adapted by other organizations in ways that Community Connections's staff perceived as inappropriate. However, given the pace of change today, organizations must learn to compete based on execution as well as intellectual property, which—despite contracts, laws, and lawyers—is increasingly difficult to protect. Especially in service-oriented businesses, success depends on implementation and relationships as much as it does on any particular delivery model.

Ambassadors play a second and key externally oriented role. They manage up and out beyond a team's or an organization's borders. This can involve helping to protect and promote the organization's reputation with external constituents, lobbying for resources, and—along with scouts—keeping in contact with potential allies, partners, and competitors. Ambassadors for a team help ensure that the team's work is aligned with the organization's priorities and gets the resources it needs from senior management. Ambassadors for an organization help ensure that its efforts fit well with changes in the environmental, regulatory, and competitive context.

Coordinators play a more task-oriented role than scouts and ensure that connections (especially lateral ones) are tight with other teams or organizations. They focus on negotiation, trading, and feedback, seeking to ensure that their group's work dovetails with the work of others. They also help ensure that their group is speaking a common language with the groups around it. In a classic example of the failure to coordinate, two groups building the Mars Climate Orbiter operated using different measurement systems until their respective parts of the rover failed, resulting in the loss of billions of dollars and thousands of hours of work. More active coordinators alone might not have saved the orbiter, but they can help fight against the tendency to become siloed and help ensure that highly interdependent work gets done smoothly.

The fourth externally oriented role is that of *guard*. It is most relevant for teams, where guards help protect members' time. They buffer the team against competing demands to ensure that members can focus on the work at hand. In flat, flexible, team-based structures, people's time can easily be "borrowed" by or shifted to other projects in ways that undermine the focal project's progress. Guards help ensure that critical resources are protected.

Is a tendency toward rigid responses always high and are these four roles always necessary to help defend against that tendency? Not always, but they are increasingly important given general trends in the environments for teams' and organizations' work. When that work requires entrepreneurship (or intrapreneurship), carefully formed alliances, buy-in and shared resources, and complex, dispersed information, keeping one's doors and windows open (albeit with "a guard on duty") is vital. CEOs are critical for ensuring that their teams and organizations don't become so heads down that they lose track of customers, clients, collaborators, and competitors. CEOs and other senior leaders can play these four roles themselves or they can assign others to play them. Either way, being carefully and continually attuned to the external environment is one of the greatest challenges (given our innate threat-rigid tendencies) and opportunities (given our increasingly inter-connected and interdependent world).

SUGGESTED READINGS

Deborah Ancona and Henrik Bresman's work on teams' external orientation is central on this topic and includes, with David Caldwell, "The X-Factor: Six Steps to Leading High-Performing X-Teams," *Organizational Dynamics* 38, no. 3 (2009): 217–24; with Katrin Käufer, "The Comparative Advantage of X-Teams," *MIT Sloan Management Review* 43, no. 3 (2002); and *X-Teams: How to Build Teams that Lead, Innovate, and Succeed* (Boston, MA: Harvard Business Review Press, 2008). They, in turn, draw on Connie Gersick and Richard Hackman's work about groups' tendency toward inwardly focused habitual routines.[14]

On the inward versus outward orientation, as well as many other topics relevant to organizations' growth and leadership, see Daniel Kahneman, *Thinking, Fast and Slow* (New York: Doubleday, 2011). For a sample model for how organizations can develop a more external perspective, see Catherine Bailey and David Butcher, "External Perspective—An Under-Utilised Strategic Leadership Capability," in *Leadership Learning: Knowledge into Action*, ed. Kim Turnbull James and James Collins, 35–55 (New York: Palgrave, 2008).

The original model and description of threat-rigidity effects for individuals, teams, and organizations is from Barry M. Staw, Lloyd Sandelands, and Jane E. Dutton, "Threat Rigidity Effects in Organizational Behavior: A Multilevel Analysis," *Administrative Science Quarterly* 26, no. 4 (1981): 501–24.

7

THE IMPORTANCE OF SELF AND ORGANIZATIONAL AWARENESS

Taking a Hard Look

Philosophies, both Eastern and Western, place great emphasis on self-awareness. At some point in its growth, an organization and its leaders need to assess where they have come from and where they are headed. Organizations may make new mistakes, but unless they engage in a process of self-awareness, they will be doomed to make the same mistakes over and over again.

We are all urged to understand just who we are. What are our strengths and how do we identify our weaknesses? How do we appear to those who see us? Much writing in philosophy, fiction, and religion, among others, stresses the importance of self-knowledge. We are warned that only the fool goes through life not knowing who he is. For some, the struggle to know oneself is the main task of their existence. We have all heard the line from Shakespeare, "To thine own self be true."[1]

But this is not a book about self-realization, or personal analysis, or individual fulfillment, so we have to ask, "What relevance does self-awareness have for running a business like Community Connections?"

A FABLE: A FACE IN THE MIRROR

"What do I look like?" asked the young boy as he and his parents were sitting in their home one evening.

"Whatever do you mean?" asked his mother with a confused look on her face. "I have never heard such a silly question."

"No, Mother, I am quite serious" he insisted with an intensity his parents had not seen before. "What do I look like?"

"Why, you look like you," said his father in a gentle voice designed to soothe his son's growing agitation.

"That is not enough," said the boy. "I have seen the face of a bear when he opens his mouth and growls and I have seen his big black tongue as he swats the bees on the way to the hive that drips with honey. I can describe the feathered birds who drink from the pond and peck for grubs on the bark of the old tree. I can describe each of these and more, but I cannot describe my own face!" The boy held his face in his hands and looked quite sad indeed.

Then he heard the voice of the old man who lived in the hills. "Your face hides in the depths of the forest and by the side of the flowing river and in the reflections that come from the sky. If you truly want to find your face, you must travel on your own for many months. And only then will you know that the face you have found will belong only to you. It will be your true face."

Even though the task seemed daunting and the time seemed long, the boy felt a sense of excitement, and with that, he packed a bag, said good-bye to his parents, and started on his way.

As he walked into the forest with the light shining behind him, he suddenly saw something on the road ahead. As he approached the dark image, he felt a surge of excitement. "That must be my face on the forest floor. He quickly bent over to grab the image, but every time he moved forward, the image of his face disappeared. "This is some trick," he cried. "I am sure that the image on the forest floor is my true face, but every time I reach over to touch it, it disappears. I know my face is here somewhere, but perhaps I must travel further before I can see it clearly."

With that thought, he headed down a path in the forest to a stream nearby. As he looked down into the water, he saw a bright, clear face looking back at him. "Wait," he cried, "that must be my face down there in the water." But just as he stood back to admire the face, the wind began to blow and a big cloud hovered above the stream. The face disappeared as a swirl of ripples churned the water, and though he waited for a long while, the face failed to reappear.

"I fear that I will never find my face," he lamented as he sat down on a shiny rock to contemplate his fate. Just as he was ready to give up his quest and return home, he looked down again and on the flat surface of the rock he saw a face staring back at him. This time the wind did not blow and the face did not disappear. "What a handsome face," he cried. But just as he was admiring the face on the rock, he heard a deep growling sound and when he looked up, he saw a big black bear, standing on his hind legs and letting out the most ferocious growl.

The boy began running until he collapsed on the forest bed. "The forces in the forest are too powerful for me. I cannot best the shadows and the clouds, or the water and the wind or the powerful voice of the big black bear; I must leave this place quickly and accept that I will never find my face."

When the boy arrived home after days of walking, his parents could see the forlorn look on his face. He tried to tell them what had happened, but he found himself choking back tears. "I have looked hard, dear parents, but I have been unable to find my true face."

Then he heard the voice of the old man in the hills. "Look into the eyes of your parents, my boy."

"But why?" asked the boy, who feared that this would be just one more disappointment.

"No," said the voice, "turn your eyes and look deeply." And there, in the eyes of his parents, was a reflection, a reflection of his own true face. "There you are," laughed the voice from the hills. "Sometimes you can find your face where you least expect it!"

The boy in the fable is searching for his "one" true face, but in any business the leaders need to wear many different faces as they deal in a multitude of circumstances. The face in the mirror may not always be the same. Remember going into the fun house as a child? One mirror makes you tall, another makes you fat, and yet another stretches out your face so that you look like you have the widest smile ever. It's a relief when you walk out of the tent and recognize your good old face. But some experiences, events, or relationships change who we are forever. Shakespeare encouraged us to remember that "A man, in his time, plays many parts."[2]

In any organization the term "self-awareness" applies in at least two places: the personal awareness of the leader or leaders and the more abstract awareness of the organization itself. It may seem a little odd to talk about the self-awareness of an organization, but organizations have identities too. They are identities based on their mission, their values, and how they operate in the world.

At a personal level, a leader needs to be aware of her strengths, her weaknesses, and her impact on others. And she must also acknowledge that every strength holds a kernel of weakness and every weakness carries a ray of strength. At an organizational level, there needs to be an awareness of where the organization has been and where it is headed. The organization needs to know its values and how its operations are viewed by others. Awareness at each level allows an organization to make good decisions about what projects to undertake, who to hire, and where it wants to be in two, three, or five years down the road.

CASE STUDY #1: AWARENESS OF INDIVIDUAL STRENGTHS

It is not surprising that this has been the hardest chapter to write. Taking an honest and deep look at ourselves is one of the most difficult things any of us has to do, yet it is necessary for running a successful business. Our choices, our decisions, our judgment are all a reflection of who we are. How we use or compensate for our core character has an enormous impact on the success or failure of the enterprise we run.

We draw our personal awareness from several places: what we have done (past); what we are doing (present); what we aspire to do (future); how we feel about what we are doing (internal); and how others see us (external).

I have always been a big picture thinker. I like to come up with new ideas. And from the beginning of my career I have always fancied myself somewhat of an intellectual. Over the years, I have written books, treatment manuals, articles, and grants, and I have presented at large local and national conferences. This litany is not meant to toot my own horn, but rather to describe how I thought and think of myself. Because of this awareness of my skills, a perception shared by others, I was given many opportunities to do what I liked and what I did well—sponsor journal clubs, run case consultations, and teach entry level clinicians. I approached many organizational concerns as problems to be solved. This strength brought many opportunities and accolades in its wake.

But behaving solely as a "big thinker" does not translate into being a good business person. It also has the unintended consequence of presenting oneself as a teacher. Some love to be in a learning environment, but for others it raises all the anxieties they hoped to escape when they got a "real" job. For others, it gave the impression that I was avoiding doing the hard work of treating clients by indulging my academic interests.

But I was also aware that I had another set of quite different strengths. I loved being a clinician and I was thought to have exceptional skills; as a result, I did something that most CEOs of health care organizations never do. I saw clients. This gave me the advantage of being able to evaluate our services firsthand. I was also seen as a hands-on leader, and clinicians knew that I was not asking them to do anything that I did not do myself. I frequently got hugs from clients as they walked into the organization and this gave the message to staff that we took our mission of providing care seriously.

CASE STUDY #2: AWARENESS OF INDIVIDUAL WEAKNESSES

These strengths, however, were coupled with a significant weakness. Even though I had a business partner whose talents I trusted, I felt great responsibility, as do many founder CEOs, for the success of Community Connections. That sense of responsibility caused me to rely too heavily on myself when making decisions and to be a bad collaborator.

There were many times when I felt a sense of urgency, often false urgency, to make a decision. Taking time for long discussions, respecting the opinion of others, and arriving at consensus all seemed like luxuries we could not afford. In leadership meetings, senior staff grew increasingly silent, believing that at the end of the day the decision would ultimately be mine. The correctness of the decision became irrelevant. Even if I was correct, the noncollaborative process resulted in a decrease in staff morale, but more important, a number of senior staff became less invested in the success of Community Connections.

But becoming aware that my style ran counter to my goal of running a successful business was difficult to accomplish. I resisted feedback and vigorously insisted that the only thing that mattered was getting it right. Only when some valued staff decided to take their talents elsewhere was I forced to take a look at what was my greatest weakness. I had to learn how to collaborate with others if I wanted Community Connections to survive and grow. I began soliciting advice from others and actually listening to the advice I received. I encouraged other senior staff to take charge of meetings and to assume authority for important parts of the business. Now there were definitely times when I had to bite my tongue, but the commitment to engaging the talents of others overrode my need to be in control. Awareness of one's weaknesses in particular needs to lead to behavior change. Otherwise, awareness can devolve into a "take it or leave it" attitude that is certainly not good for the longevity of any business.

CASE STUDY #3: AWARENESS OF ONE'S IMPACT ON OTHERS

Being aware of one's personal strengths and weaknesses is only one part of the process of gaining and sustaining awareness. The second level is to be aware of how your behavior impacts the behavior of others. For years, Community Connections held a big gala at Christmastime. Staff had a chance to dress up and go dancing at an upscale venue. Over the years, as the size of the staff grew, the cost of the event also escalated. The leaders decided to suspend the event and to give each team a budget for a much smaller and more intimate affair of their own. We were unaware of how important the event had become for many staff. In fact, when new employees were hired, some of their colleagues would say, "Just wait till Christmas, the organization has a really great party." All the leaders could see was the cost of the event—not what it meant to staff. The lack of awareness caused staff to feel that leadership was unfeeling and too cheap to treat them to a Christmas celebration.

Understanding your own behavior is only half of the equation. Understanding how your behavior will impact others explains much of what happens in organizations.

CASE STUDY # 4: THE PRISON OF THE PERSONA

Self-awareness and an awareness of the expectations of others can actually feel like a prison at times. People expect certain behaviors of leaders, and the need to conform to those expectations can be stifling. The situation can be doubly burdensome when the expectations match expectations leaders have of themselves. In its early years, leaders at Community Connections held an end of the year appreciation event.

At the event, the cofounders would personally distribute bonuses to staff who were part of the senior team as a way of both rewarding them for a year of hard work and honoring their contribution to the organization's success. The bonuses, which were quite substantial and were given in cash (a practice that was abandoned when the tax implications became clear), made the employees feel valued but also contributed to the persona, shared by the cofounders about themselves, of the leaders as powerful and generous.

One year, one of the cofounders broke her leg before the event, making her unable to participate with the same flair that had been her style. Rather than skipping the event, or allowing her partner to handle the gift-giving alone, the founder in question insisted that she be wheeled around the room in a borrowed wheelchair! She felt bound to maintain her image as a strong leader, needing to show her staff that nothing could stop her, not even a broken leg. She was aware of her persona and of how others viewed her, so she felt bound to stay in her role regardless of how she felt in the moment.

Organizational Awareness

Organizations are not people, but they do have identities. Some businesses may be viewed as cutthroat by the competition; others might be seen as collaborative or more cautious in their decision-making style. Organizations that are viewed as cutthroat may turn off mild-mannered albeit competent potential employees; orgaizations seen as sluggish and slow to react may invite aggressive action from competitors. In a slightly different vein, an organization's internal awareness of its culture may impact the opportunities it opts to pursue and the applicants it chooses to hire and promote.

Organizational identity derives from both its values and its history. Values may be articulated explicitly in a mission statement, but they may also be reflected in how the company does business. Organizations, like people, go through a series of developmental changes. Awareness of those changes and how they impact the ongoing success of a business contributes to its identity.

CASE STUDY #5: ORGANIZATIONAL VALUES

Community Connection has always identified itself as a mission-driven organization. We serve the mental and behavioral health needs of marginalized individuals who live with social, emotional, and physical disabilities. Yet beyond the commitment to delivering quality care, most of our values involved style rather than content. We were firm that we believed in respect and equality for both clients and staff, and we strove to demonstrate integrity in all that we did.

Several years after we first opened, we had a chance to look back over these values and we were surprised. We looked like the solid "good guy" organization, but we could have been delivering any service. We could have been a school or a legal aid society or any of a number of socially minded organizations. Our core purpose seemed eclipsed by a focus on style, on process rather than content.

At one point, we were asked by one of our funders to reassess the clinical needs of a group of clients and to discharge those who no longer met the criteria of medical necessity. When we looked at our treatment philosophy this made sense. We believed in teaching people skills and moving them to greater independence. We even designed treatments to help people overcome disabling symptoms. What if a client did not want to be discharged? How could we hold to our value of respecting client wishes while at the same time delivering recovery-focused treatment?

We eventually realized that in defining ourselves we had gotten confused as to what was the figure and what was the ground. Our mission of delivering quality services was our foreground and our values formed the background, but, as in figure ground puzzles, if you look at them a certain way the foreground and background begin to reverse. At one point Community Connections spent more time and gave more weight to being a respectful organization than it did to being an organization that delivered behavioral health services. This reversal is not uncommon in many social service agencies where "good guy" values can come to trump core mission.

CASE STUDY #6: PAST, PRESENT, AND FUTURE

Who we are depends on where we have been, what we have accomplished, and how we see our future. In the beginning, Community Connections saw itself and was seen by others as "the little engine that could." With few resources and a small staff, the organization took on projects that others, even the local government, found daunting. Unfortunately, there were times when the organization bought its own publicity and reached for opportunities that were just too big for it to handle. At one point Community Connections bid for and was awarded a large federal grant that involved enrolling hundreds of clients over a short span of time. We did not have adequate staff, prior experience, nor had we done a careful assessment of just who the clients were. Our venture failed and we ultimately needed to pull out of the project and return the funding. We were aware of the positive side of our can do attitude, but we were not aware of all that we needed to learn.

Some years later, in our development as a behavioral treatment center, we recognized that many of our clients were in need of very practical resources: safe housing, secure employment, enough money for food and basic necessities. In addition to offering traditional behavioral health care, we began providing a full range of housing and employment services. For a time this created somewhat of an identity crisis. We would get calls asking if we had low-cost housing available or if we could help someone find a job. We became aware that our desire to provide a full range of recovery services had caused people outside of the organization to mistake who we were. A number of arguments and complaints resulted as we attempted to clarify our core mission.

Using our past experiences, we continue the ongoing process of restating and clarifying just who we are and what we do. We are clear that we see ourselves as a full service behavioral health organization, but we have returned to putting "behavioral" health back in the center of our identity. It is true that we want to serve people with respect and dignity. And we continue to strive to provide all the services that individuals need in order to survive in a multifaceted community. But we do all of these in the context of a strengths-based behavioral health recovery model.

Recently we have been judged by funders on how well we can describe what we do. A number of young clinicians put activities like finding housing and getting people to appointments at the center of how they describe their activities. While these are valuable services, they are not behavioral health services. We have needed to remind our staff and ourselves of just what our core mission is. Our clear awareness that we are a behavioral health organization has helped us satisfy our funders and make better choices about what new opportunities we want to pursue.

As we look to the future, we are aware that our identity will need to change once again. Health care is changing and we need to keep pace with those changes. We need to integrate behavioral health care with primary health care services. We now see some of our relationship building efforts as ways to help people better manage their physical health. This does not mean that we are changing our core mission or betraying our values. What it does reflect, however, is that organizational awareness has to include an awareness of the context in which the business exists. This broader awareness will help us make better choices and clearer decisions as we go forward.

Knowing who you are at both a personal and organizational level is essential for success. It guides the choices you make, the partners you seek, and the challenges you assume. Almost every mistake we have made at Community Connections grew out of our lack of awareness about what talents and capacities we had. Sometimes we took on too much and at other times we did not stretch ourselves far enough.

Knowing who we are also helps us to understand our impact on others. How we are seen has a great impact on the kind of deal we can negotiate. When we operate from a position of power, we are likely to come away with a different resolution than when we are seen as fearful or damaged. But we are in an even better position when we know how we are seen and we know how much this matches with our own awareness of who we are. The Trojan horse was seen by the Trojans as a big wooden structure, a trophy of their triumph over the Greeks. That mistaken awareness resulted in their pulling the horse inside the gates. The Greeks inside the horse knew that they would have the advantage if the horse was pulled inside. As it turned out, the awareness of the Trojans was mistaken. The Greeks were not only aware of their own prowess, they were aware of the mistake the Trojans had made and thus of their own ability to fool the enemy and emerge victorious. To paraphrase Plato, "the unexamined life" may not only be unworthy of living, it may also get you into a lot of trouble![3]

Despite this justifiable praise for the value of self-awareness, there is, however, one caveat. It is possible to be too aware. If David had been aware that his chances of victory were slim, he might not have challenged the mighty Goliath. It was only his lack of self-awareness that allowed him to take up his slingshot. There are some risks we might refuse to take, risks with a high upside, if we were fully aware of the odds. In the words of the singer-songwriter Bob Seger, "I wish I didn't know now what I didn't know then."[4]

A PERSONAL NOTE FROM MAXINE

At one point I decided to give staff a chance to think out loud about Community Connections and its values. I held a series of meetings in which I remained silent and let young staff do the talking. The events were a disaster. Just because I liked to talk and think out loud, I assumed that others would feel the same. I ignored the fact that there was a great power differential between me and the staff I invited. They were naturally afraid to voice their thoughts to the boss. And to make matters worse, I failed to set an agenda for the meeting, thinking that an open-ended format would be best.

My lack of awareness regarding the potential impact of my behavior led to a series of tense meetings. Participants left feeling inadequate, demeaned, and used. They wondered if I had a secret agenda, perhaps to evaluate their performance. My failure to understand the impact of my seemingly well-meaning behavior led to months of distrust and the lingering feeling on the part of some that Community Connections was a hostile organization. One woman in particular was so upset that she chose to write me a letter after she left Community Connections and took another job. In the letter she lambasted me for being a smug, insensitive boss. She said I set the tone for an uncaring and harsh organization. She was so afraid that I might retaliate that she signed her letter Anonymous and gave her address as Yankee Stadium. I felt so ashamed that I have never forgotten that letter.

PUTTING SELF-AWARENESS AT COMMUNITY CONNECTIONS IN CONTEXT

The fable and preceding case examples address the importance of self-awareness—both in terms of one's strengths and one's weaknesses. In this final section of the chapter, we highlight the best and latest social science regarding self-awareness, which is one of the core components of emotional intelligence. Because people are not generally very accurate in their self-awareness, it limits their likelihood of getting (or accepting) helpful feedback or of making good choices in terms of their own learning and development.

There are many ways in which our own well-meaning brains trip us up when we try to gauge our own skills, abilities, and character. Generally, there is only a meager to modest correlation between our self-assessments and others' assessments of us.[5] It is statistically impossible for the average person to be "above average," but that its what the average person believes he or she is. This tendency is quite broad and general, with applications in health care, education, business, and every other context.

It has come to be known as the Kruger-Dunning effect—named after the psychologists credited with the early and most influential work on it.[6] In some of their studies, for example, Kruger and Dunning found that those in the 12th percentile (on tests of things as varied as humor, grammar, and logic) estimated that they'd be in the 62nd percentile.[7] This basic finding, that poor performers grossly overestimate their performance, has been replicated and extended now numerous times—in the real world and even with explicit incentives for people to be accurate.

The challenge of accurate self-assessment seems especially significant for those with low ability in a given domain, but the challenge applies to health professionals and others who would generally be considered high ability. For example, dozens of studies show that physicians have a limited ability to accurately self-assess. In studies of other professions (including law, engineering, counseling, and psychology), the average correlation between self- and external assessments was 0.39. College professors aren't immune either—94 percent think they're above average![8]

Correlations between our self-assessments and others' assessments of us vary, but are all within a very low band for a wide variety of outcomes. Across numerous studies and multiple domains, the average correlation between self-perception and objective measures is less than 0.30.[9] In specific domains, the correlations vary but are still quite low. The exceptions tend to be domains like sports where there is frequent, more objective feedback. For example, typical correlations between self- and others' assessments are shown below:

- .04 for self vs. supervisor ratings of performance on managerial competence;
- .17 for self vs. supervisor ratings of interpersonal skills;
- .20 for self vs. supervisor performance on complex workplace tasks;
- .30 for self-assessments vs. tests of intelligence;
- .35 for first year students' vs. professors' ratings of their academic abilities; and,
- .47 for self vs. other ratings in athletic performance.[10]

Relatively inexperienced peers' and supervisors' ratings are better than students' own predictions of their performance on medical exams.[11] Peer ratings are better than naval officers' ratings at predicting their selection for promotion to leadership roles.[12] Somewhat frightening, even *strangers* can do nearly as well at predicting our intelligence (based on only ninety-second video clips of us reading weather reports) as we can at predicting our own intelligence.[13] Taken together, these statistics are sobering—perhaps triggering an ironic tendency to underestimate our tendency to overestimate.

Across those studies, the tendency toward poor self-assessment was not linked to training levels, specialties, or domains of self-assessment. It also appears to be problematic in retrospect (How accurately do I judge my past performance?), in the moment (How well can I identify my current needs or performance deficits?), and in a predictive way (How well do I predict my future performance?). Poor self-assessment (and especially overconfidence) is a fundamental barrier to improvement—for individuals, teams, and organizations. If we can't accurately assess our strengths and weaknesses, we cannot address them effectively. Before noting ways to defend against these tendencies, we summarize what's known about their sources.

SOURCES OF THE GAPS IN OUR SELF-ASSESSMENT

Why do others know us better than we know ourselves? Fundamentally, the gaps in our self-assessment are a function of a lack of information or our tendency to neglect available information. We lack situational details and overemphasize our own specific experience (essentially responding more to our own case example than to the broader statistical probabilities). We also neglect alternative scenarios, concrete details, background circumstances, and the lessons of experience.[14] Importantly for our understanding of life in organizations, these information deficits are the result of workplace feedback that is often infrequent, poorly timed, threatening, and less than candid. In addition, in many fields, it is difficult to define competence. The more specific the trait, the better our self-assessments tend to be.[15]

WAYS TO ENHANCE THE QUALITY OF OUR SELF-ASSESSMENTS

It is not easy to overcome our inability to self-assess well, but there are ways to improve the probability that we size ourselves up in ways that are more consistent with objective evidence and others' judgments of us. Changes in feedback content and processes are the primary means by which we can improve our self-assessments. First, when we get feedback closer in time to the behavior that triggered the feedback, it has a stronger effect on our self-assessments (and our future behavior). This recognition has been a factor in large companies' recent shifts toward "micro" feedback—given on a daily, weekly, or task basis—rather than annual or semiannual reviews, when the feedback comes so long after the behavior that people struggle to incorporate it into their future actions. Second, the more personalized feedback is, the greater the effect on people's self-assessments. For example, when clients receive data on their individual risk profiles, they tend to be more realistic about the probability of having a stroke than if they just receive information about the general risk factors.[16] Third, our self-assessments are likely to improve when we get feedback from people who are somewhat removed—and thus more objective—about our work. Pushing people to pay attention to and give greater weight to environmental signals in general improves their self-assessments.

Getting useful feedback can be a dyadic undertaking—between the feedback seeker and the feedback provider—but it can also be something that is ingrained in the culture of the organization. It can be done in a way that doesn't just involve more reviews. Creating 360 degree review processes have become monsters that consume more time and energy than their potential benefits warrant. The more that feedback is done on a small, regular basis, the less cumbersome it is—and the more likely people will actually give and receive it well. If feedback is only something that happens in response to major problems, or only happens on an annual basis, it is less likely that people will give good, candid feedback, and less likely that people will be able to act on it. The more that giving and receiving regular feedback (regardless of rank or status) is part of everyone's normal expectations—that is, that we ask for and receive good feedback—and the less we have to formally schedule it, the more useful it becomes. As with all feedback, the closer in time that it comes to the work, the more valuable it is for people and groups who want to improve that work. In addition, the more psychologically safe the team or organization is, the more likely people will be able to give, receive, and act on feedback effectively.

When feedback becomes a normal part of the culture, it also helps the organization stay more generally aware of its environment. See chapter 6 for a more detailed discussion of environmental awareness.

SUGGESTED READINGS

Self-awareness is a topic with fuzzy boundaries and many fields that shed light on it. Camille Sweeney and Josh Gosfield's book *The Art of Doing: How Superachievers Do What They Do and How They Do It So Well* (New York: Penguin, 2013) provides an interesting look at people who got to the top of their fields in part because they did the hard work of striving to be self-aware. Another good, reflective starting point is the chapter titled "Self-Awareness," by former Novartis CEO Daniel Vasella in Gary Burnison's *No Fear of Failure: Real Stories of How Leaders Deal with Risk and Change* (San Francisco, CA: Jossey-Bass, 2011). Other chapters in that book are instructive as well.

There are many books and articles about how to give and receive feedback effectively. Doug Stone's *Thanks for the Feedback: The Science and Art of Receiving Feedback Well* (New York: Penguin, 2015) is an excellent starting point on the receiving side. Kerry Patterson and Joseph Grenny's *Crucial Conversations: Tools for Talking When Stakes Are High* (New York: McGraw-Hill, 2012) addresses how to create a safe environment for effective feedback; so do chapters 5 and 6 in Amy Edmondson's excellent *Teaming: How Organizations Learn, Innovate, and Compete in the Knowledge Economy* (San Francisco, CA: Jossey-Bass, 2012).

8

PREPARING FOR THE FUTURE

What's Next?

Even in a relatively young organization, leaders need to have one eye to the future. To some it may seem premature, or even downright silly, to plan for sustaining an organization that has not been fully developed. But so many founder-run organizations fail to survive into the next generation. While a full-fledged plan may be unnecessary, understanding what lies ahead is not.

A FABLE: LITTLE ONE NOTE

For years, the clan had lived safely in the valley behind the tall trees of the forest. There was plenty of space for each family to have its own lodge and the forest was filled with enough game so that hunting was easy and a full pot brimmed with stew over every fireplace. There was never any fighting, because there was more than enough for everyone.

But after a while, as is the case with families, the number of children multiplied and the space in the valley had to be shared with more and more people. Families squabbled with one another, mothers grew angry with their children, and hunters began to question whether neighbors were poaching deer and rabbits from their part of the forest.

After many years, as the problem grew worse, the chief of the clan spoke in a loud voice. "Our beloved valley is now too small to hold all of our people. If we are once again to live in peace, we must move to a larger valley with more plentiful forests. There is such a valley across the hills, but we will need to walk very far and it will take many days."

"No! No!" cried the families. "We cannot leave behind all that we have known and everything that we have built and nurtured. We will stay here." But despite their efforts and their attempts to make do, the problems only grew worse. So once again the chief called his people together and told them that they must move. This time, some of the younger clansmen saw the wisdom of his words.

"If we move, we will see new things and face new challenges. We will become a bigger and stronger clan."

"Yes! Yes!" others cried. "We will follow our chief and move to the valley over the hills." And with that, the members of the clan began to pack up their belongings and prepare to move. But there was not enough room on the caravans and wagons; some things would need to be left behind.

As the families started sorting, and saving and discarding, they also began remembering all of the ceremonies and joys, all the rituals and tragedies that had been part of their lives in the valley.

In the midst of all the activity, however, one little girl (who was known as "Little One Note") could be heard whimpering. Little One Note (who was called this because she was always the one to sound the note of caution whenever a decision needed to be made) came to her mother with a handful of her dolls and her clothing and the lucky stones she had collected from the riverbed. "How can I leave without all of my treasures? It has taken me my whole life to collect them and now I must leave some behind. Things will never be the same. I just know it!"

Despite Little One Note's fears and worries, the clan began its passage from one valley to the next. The journey took longer and was far harder than anyone had expected, and some valued items were indeed lost along the way. But when the families began settling into their new home, they could all see the wisdom of the old chief. All except for Little One Note, who continued to believe that it would have been better to stay in the old valley.

For many, many years, the members of the clan lived peacefully, with much space and plenty of game to hunt. Of course, things were not exactly as they had been. More space meant that clan members were more spread out, and it took more effort for children to play with old *friends and for mothers to share in the chores and the daily gossip. They also needed more rules, for after all, so many people cannot live together without rules to keep them safe.*

While most of the clan members were happy with life in the bigger valley, some longed for the simpler life they had known and so they split off to find a smaller clan where they might return to the old ways. Little One Note, who was now a grown woman with children of her own, continued to worry that the clan had made a big mistake.

It is funny how growth seems to lead to more growth, for after many years, the clan had grown too big for the valley over the hills. When the same chief, who was now very, very old and who had seen many things, called his people together, everyone expected him to offer the same solution as he had before, that the clan must move to yet a bigger valley. But no . . .

"My people, we have surely grown to be such a large and powerful clan that we can no longer all live in this valley together. We do not need to move as one, but we will need to split off a group of our bravest families and have them build a new village close to the one we already have. They will become our worthy neighbors and we will trade with them and join with them to celebrate the coming of each new moon."

As you might expect, Little One Note fell back with fear and worry. "I knew it. The chief has made a plan that will destroy our clan. We have flourished and lived well in this valley. We have learned to trust and respect one another and now the chief will ruin everything that we have accomplished." (Of course Little One Note had completely forgotten that she was the one who had objected to the move to the bigger valley in the first place.)

It took much planning and discussion, but finally the move of the chosen families began. Even though they were going only a small distance away, there were many good-byes to be said and many promises to be made. They all knew that distance would change things.

Little One Note sat alone with a worried look on her face until her young daughter came to her side and took her hand, "Why are you always so fearful and concerned that change will bring tragedy? I do not understand, dear mother."

At which point Little One Note broke into a big smile (something she did not often do). "I will tell you a secret, which you must never repeat. For generations upon generations, our clan has always had a 'Little One

Note,' someone to be the voice of caution and warning. Just as singing and dancing and harvesting and cooking have been our ways, so too is the voice of 'Little One Note.' So hush now and go to sleep, and remember, it is a secret."

Organizations need to grow and move and change if they are to survive. While there are always some, like Little One Note in the fable, who are afraid of moving on, most of the clan can see the necessity, and even the adventure, of trying something new. But something new does not mean that old rituals and values get left behind. The trick to growth and longevity is to find ways to get bigger, to sustain the organization that you have, and to plan for a healthy future.

CASE STUDY #1: SCALABILITY

Scalability is the capacity of an organization to expand its core business. Several factors allowed Community Connections to grow its clinical services and therefore its revenue from a small three-person operation into the biggest not-for-profit behavioral health care organization in the nation's capital. This scaling up happened in several ways.

We took our core business, providing community-based mental health services for marginalized individuals, and we just did more of it. At the beginning we had three employees, thirty-five clients, and one clinical team. As business increased, we created a second team, and then a third, and so on until by our thirtieth anniversary, we had upward of ten teams. But now, the teams consisted of ten case managers and three hundred clients. In order to maintain the flow of clients, we streamlined our intake process, adding a specialized department whose sole responsibility was to make sure that clients could enter our system easily. We also set up a grievance process so that unhappy clients could have their concerns addressed, making it likely that they would continue to receive their services at Community Connections.

But scaling up meant more than just increasing the size of our core business; the more we worked with individuals, the more we could see that their needs extended beyond mental health services. They also needed treatment for addictions, homelessness, chronic unemployment, the social and behavioral impact of HIV, the long-term effects of domestic violence and childhood trauma, and repeated criminal justice involvement. Our recognition of these additional needs also corresponded to local and national mandates to provide problem-specific services.

Growth meant adding several new service components that both overlapped and rivaled our core business. New treatments also meant new and different clients. We were able to reach out to people being diverted from the criminal justice system, men and women living in homeless shelters, and displaced families, among others. The business grew as we grew our initial mission to serve mental and behavioral health needs.

As we added new services and became adept at new clinical interventions, we also recognized that our services need not be limited to adults. With some modifications, we began providing care to families and children, and we began to grow as we addressed their special problems, teenage pregnancy, foster care, the reliance on insufficient entitlement programs, and substandard housing. Without much shift in our core model, we were in a position to scale up when the opportunity presented itself.

In order to be in a position to increase our business, we rid ourselves, or prepared to rid ourselves, of costly administrative services that we were providing in-house. For example, as residential services became an increasingly large part of our portfolio, we found ourselves owning almost forty homes and apartment buildings that needed managing. At first we opted to manage these properties in-house, creating a housing management department that needed staff and access to equipment and specialized craftsmen and assumed the risk for property damage. When we purchased a new property, the management department had to learn the ins and outs of how to manage the new building. They had to assess the repairs needed and the amenities required, as well as the permits necessary to occupy the building. There were times when this process took months. By divesting ourselves of the task of managing property, we were able to move much more nimbly when we wanted to add new properties to our existing portfolio.

The ability to scale up quickly also meant that we needed partners, collaborators who would bring new capacities and new funding streams into our organization. For the most part, those partners were universities or other public clinics. We partnered with Dartmouth University to design a program for adults dually diagnosed with a mental illness and a substance abuse disorder, and together we applied for and were awarded federal grant money that ranged from $500,000 to $2.5 million over several years. It was amazing how quickly we could grow our business with new money and a new level of expertise, and money seemed to breed more money. Over time, we became known as an organization that could ramp up services quickly and deliver a quality product.

Two other variables that may seem less related to our clinical services facilitated our ability to grow quickly: the use of space and the use of personnel. When Community Connections first opened, clinicians worked in individual, separate offices whenever possible. That meant having one office for every clinician hired. As time went on, offices were shared by two clinicians, but in essence adding services meant adding clinicians and adding clinicians meant adding office space, which is a very costly way to grow. It became obvious that this model was unsustainable. We could never afford all the space we would need. At the suggestion of an architect, we moved away from individual offices. Clinicians shared open space with computers and cubicles placed on moveable workstations. Adding staff frequently required the addition of no new space at all, and staff were encouraged to share informal conversations, which meant that many clinicians had information that would allow them to serve the same client. Services could take place even when the primary clinician was out of the office, making overall practice more efficient.

Changing who we hired also made it easier for us to scale up quickly. Initially, Community Connections only hired licensed clinicians: social workers, psychologists, and counselors. These practitioners were expensive, at times difficult to find, and sometimes frustrated with the tediousness of the work. A closer look at some of our contracts suggested that we could easily provide the services with less highly trained staff. This did not mean that we would sacrifice quality; what it did mean, however, was that we would hire young staff, often recent college graduates, who were eager to learn and passionate about serving people who had multiple needs. We would still hire some more trained, licensed staff, but only for those positions that required specialized skills. This shift in hiring philosophy meant that we always had a large pool of applicants from which to choose and could therefore start new programs quickly.

And finally, Community Connections was able to grow quickly because it got lucky. It just so happened to open its doors during a time of little competition. There were very few other organizations interested in working with the same group of clients. When new opportunities arose, Community Connections was often the only organization ready to take them on.

CASE STUDY #2: SUSTAINABILITY

It is one thing to be able to grow quickly, but it is quite another to be able to sustain that growth into the future. Several different variables contributed to Community Connections's longevity.

Responding to the "Winds of Change"

In every business environment, there are forces outside of the business that bring about sweeping change. For Community Connections, change came every time an election brought in a new municipal administration that held the power to change behavioral health priorities. Over the course of several years, the emphasis shifted from working with chronically mentally ill individuals, to finding supportive housing for homeless men and women, to working with families and children, and then back again. An organization needed to understand the changing priorities and be ready to provide new services quickly. This did not mean that we abandoned old priorities, but it did mean that we accepted, and at times even embraced, change.

The environment also changed as new competitors came into the market. We could no longer assume that all the business would come our way. By forging relationships, joining in partnerships with other providers, and quite frankly listening to gossip, we were able to adapt to a changing environment before new priorities made our business obsolete.

Expanding the Focus of Care

When it first opened, Community Connections's services were focused on single adults. The first wave of clients were coming out of institutions where they had been accustomed to receiving full service care—psychiatric and physical care all in one place. Community Connections, however, was only mandated to provide behavioral and mental health services in order to help people live independently and better cope with stressful circumstances. The focus was on single individuals and on psychiatric symptoms. Any attention to physical health was pushed into the background. It was as if the client had been split into two halves, a mental self and a physical self.

By the mid to late 1990s, the focus within the health care system began to shift and practitioners were beginning to see the client as a whole person.[1] Community Connections had been a pioneer in seeing people as having multiple issues in multiple domains simultaneously—a trauma survivor with an addiction, someone with depression who was also homeless, and a variety of other comorbidities, but we, like many behavioral health care providers, kept mental and physical health separate.

The explosion of the AIDS epidemic eventually pushed many providers to see that physical health had serious mental health consequences. Community Connections applied for grants that specifically targeted people with mental and behavioral health problems who were also living with HIV or AIDS. But Community Connections went much further and adopted a more whole person approach to client care. Efforts were made to provide primary health care onsite for Community Connections clients and to open a pharmacy in the organization's main building. Relationships were forged with primary care providers and eventually a coordinated service model emerged. Community Connections's ability to recognize that the focus of care was moving toward an integrated model allowed it to grow and expand at a time when some of its competitors were contracting. As local and national mandates began to focus on integrating care, Community Connections was poised to scale its operations up because it had already seen and been prepared for a shift in focus from strict mental health services to whole person services.

Building a Strong Bench

In order to survive, any organization needs to have a farm system, people at different levels with emerging skills who are ready to assume leadership. This move into positions of greater authority may happen quickly, as when someone leaves unexpectedly, or gradually, as an existing supervisor assumes a new position at the organization. Community Connections nurtured its bench in two different ways. First, we created a junior leadership position on all of the teams that served high need clients. The junior leader spent up to a year learning the activities of the job and preparing to assume full leadership. When a junior leader was promoted, another clinician was selected to take their place, so at any one time there was a pipeline of trained people who could became supervisors.

The organization also selected twenty people who seemed to have the skills to assume greater programmatic and organizational responsibility and sent them to a three-month certificate program at Georgetown University that focused on executive leadership. Each of the twenty staff had a chance to learn and practice the skills they would need to be supervisors, managers, and leaders at Community Connections. In order to sustain the organization long after founders and original directors retired, Community Connections put effort into ensuring that it would have the necessary talent to go forward and meet new challenges.

Investing in the Next Best Thing

An organization cannot sustain itself by doing the same thing over and over again. While Community Connections devoted time and energy to establishing its brand, providing local and national training, and developing marketable products, it probably did more for its long-term viability by being able to discern the next best thing—the innovation that would open up the market to new businesses. There were several times when this happened—recognizing the value of peer-delivered services, seeing the impact that trauma and violence had across generations, and embracing the movement to integrate primary and behavioral health care.

In each case, the organization took the risk of investing personnel, space, and resources into a business that was not yet generating money.

In the case of integrated care, we were so sure that health care was headed in that direction that we invested in a program that went a year without reaching profitability. Obviously, you have to know when you have made a poor investment and when it is time to pull resources out of a venture that is not succeeding, but taking risks, betting on the future, is one way in which Community Connections has been able to sustain its growth.

Staying True to the Organization's Core Mission and Values

With the change in reimbursement model, leadership struggled with how to reconcile our core mission of providing care to marginalized individuals with the necessity to make enough money to fund our efforts. The phrase "No margin, no mission" has been repeated so many times that its origin with Sister Irene Kraus of the Daughters of Charity and eventual chairperson of the American Hospital Association Board of Trustees has probably been forgotten.[2] But the phrase was intended to show how smart business practices did not mean sacrificing one's mission; in fact, mission could not exist without good fiscal management.

It took quite an effort to convince staff at Community Connections that we could remain true to our identity while still paying attention to making money. Eventually top leadership came up with a paradigm that connected clinical thinking with good care and with practical application. Called Think (T) Clinically (C) Act (A) Practically (P), TCAP helped young, idealistic staff see how direct care could be viewed as a billable clinical activity. Teaching clinicians how to operate within a TCAP framework became part of staff orientation and eventually part of the culture of Community Connections. Senior leadership also brought in a financial consultant to help managers understand how balanced budgets were critical to being able to deliver and sustain quality care.

It would be misleading to say that all staff bought into the TCAP model and the focus on maintaining billable hours. Some left, believing that Community Connections had lost its way. But most embraced the idea that our mission remained constant and that without a solid fiscal foundation our mission would soon disappear like a cloud on a windy day.

CASE STUDY #3: SUCCESSION

When Harris and Bergman opened Community Connections in 1984, succession was the last thing on their minds. They were in their mid-thirties, had an organization to run, and just assumed that Community Connections would go on and then one day it wouldn't. Bergman used to joke that one day she would just sneak out the back door, leaving her good-bye cake on the conference room table, and that would be the end of that.

The board consisted of family and two close friends and their collective goal was to help the founders be successful, not to help them plan for what would happen when they stepped down. After the sudden death of Bergman in the summer of 2011, it became obvious that a more active board with subcommittees to deal with finance and hiring were essential. New board members were added, bringing specialized expertise to help guide the remaining CEO in making better decisions for the organization. Attorneys were also engaged to establish policies and procedures for board functioning.

Senior leadership also received guidance and rewrote policies and procedures detailing how the organization should be run. Policy manuals were written and standard practices were established in the human resources and quality assurance departments. The goal was to ensure that Community Connections would have a solid structure that would allow it to survive regardless of who was running the organization.

Two of the things that were most difficult involved establishing an organizational chart for the organization and writing a clear job description for the CEO. In founder-run businesses, there is a laissez-faire attitude that almost borders on sloppiness. Who reports to whom may vary frequently, with little rationale for why things have changed. At one point, Community Connections had a chart that stretched out over a fourth of the CEO's office. The number of horizontal and vertical lines made it hard to understand just how departments were organized. Only with the help of outside coaches did the senior management devise a true organizational chart, but even then the resistance was palpable. An organizational chart is essential for CEO succession planning, and it may be best to get outside help for accomplishing the task. Only someone who can stand at a fifty foot altitude may be able to see what is really going on.

What is even more difficult perhaps is writing a job description for the CEO. Founders often run by the seat of their pants. They do a little bit of everything and like to know what is going on in all sectors of the organization. At Community Connections, we had set up a structure that would be hard to replicate. The two founders divided the functions of running the organization between themselves. The division was based on who could do certain tasks better and who liked to do certain things more. A real assessment of the skills involved in running different aspects of the business was never done. It was a model that would have been hard to replicate.

Serious CEO succession planning requires a clear job description, a delineation of necessary skills, a method for evaluating those skills, and a procedure for actual hiring. There is a reason why the U.S. government has a reliable and predictable plan for succession should something happen to the president. Within a matter of minutes, the vice president is sworn in. No one needs to fear anarchy and chaos. Even though the political analogy may seem a bit hyperbolic, the truth is, planning and structure prevent the populace (employees) from panicking.

These words may sound a bit frightening, but every founder-run organization needs a "drop dead" plan. What happens if, as it did at Community Connections, a founder dies suddenly? There is no time to train or interview a new candidate for the position of CEO. Someone needs to be identified who will step in to run the organization while a new person is hired. This did not mean that we would have several CEOs-in-waiting, but it did mean that many people would have a good understanding of how the organization and its many parts fit together and people at every level would have input into how the organization should run.

The senior management began to share knowledge. As new policies were put into place within the city and important decisions about health care were being made, it was essential that more of Community Connections key staff be involved. Never again would important information be held by just a few.

Community Connections began to operate with more of a senior leadership team. Several staff, at all levels of the organization, were involved in decision making. Discussion forums known as "All Minds Matter" were held weekly with membership set up outside of team boundaries so that more people got to know one another. These groups were designed to solicit ideas from multiple staff members.

All staff would be introduced to the administrative personnel who operated behind the scenes to keep Community Connections running smoothly. For example, a member of the IT team collaborated with a member of the addictions program to facilitate a better practice for reporting services. And a staff member from the day services program met with the head of quality assurance to design a program that would reduce risk at the organization. As hard as it is to believe, these departments had rarely talked with one another before.

Fortunately for Community Connections, a new spirit began to emerge. It was very similar to the can-do optimism that characterized Community Connections in its infancy. We rediscovered the power of why we had started Community Connections in the first place. The mission that infused the start of Community Connections was passed to a new generation of leaders with the hope that they had the tools to pass it forward after their time of leadership was done.

Like the two girls in the story, Community Connections's success has come from acknowledging the complexity in the growing organization itself, appreciating the changes in the outside world, and adapting to both. As the girls in the fable from chapter 1 say, "There will always be new games to play" and new challenges to overcome.

A PERSONAL NOTE FROM MAXINE

At the time of his son's death in the spring of 2016, then vice president Joe Biden commented that success was when your children turn out better than you.[3] I guess if Community Connections exceeded the early expectations that Helen and I set out for it, we could consider the organization and ourselves as having achieved success. But for many years we did not feel that way. We individually and together did not want Community Connections to be better after we had gone than it was when we were running things.

When Helen would talk about slipping out the back door as we retired, she also remarked that the place would slip into a comfortable mediocrity without us. I don't think that this is what she wanted or what

I hoped for; she just assumed that would be the reality—an era would come to an end and that would be okay.

It took a while after Helen's death for me to realize that mediocrity was not what I wanted to leave behind. Biden was right; my success would indeed be measured by how creative and forward thinking the organization was after I left. It was with that realization that I set out to nurture a core of new leaders who would take the organization in new directions—directions that were called for by a new future. Their success would ultimately be the best success that I could ask for.

PUTTING SCALABILITY, SUSTAINABILITY, AND SUCCESSION AT COMMUNITY CONNECTIONS IN CONTEXT

The fable and cases in the preceding sections address three fundamental issues: scalability, sustainability, and succession. In this section, we put those three issues in their broader context—highlighting some of the latest research on each. Note that sustainability in this sense refers to the long-run survival of the organization, not its environmental practices.

Scalability

In addition to succession and sustainability, this chapter's fable and first case study address the issue of scaling and scalability of organizations. In short, this refers to the process and ability of organizations to expand their existing model to serve a broader audience of clients or customers. In the process, the model may need to change some, but our focus here is on taking a basic model and extending its reach, rather than developing new models for new audiences.

Whereas success early in an organization's life is often based on the talents of a charismatic leader and/or visionary entrepreneur, growing beyond early success is a function of organizational infrastructure and financial resources. Organizationally, teamwork, focus, and metrics are crucial. Financially, the organization must be generating enough capital to grow, or must be stable enough to convince others to invest their capital to support its growth.

Of the organizational and financial keys to scaling success identified by Bob Sutton, Huggy Rao, and others, several are especially relevant to organizations like Community Connections.[4] First, doing more means doing less. Adding resources is not the only recipe for growth. This paradox is central to growing any organization. In order to scale, organizations have to focus and—sometimes—trim. Giving up traditions built during the early days and cutting ties with early employees, customers, and other constituents can be extremely difficult, but it's also necessary. For leadership teams, being able to say "We need to do more of X" requires being able to say "And we will make that possible partly by doing less of Y."

Second, create a sense of ownership and being owned. If early employees feel like they are owners, buy into the founding mindset, and hold themselves and others accountable to clear goals and metrics (including ones that reinforce core organizational values), the resulting culture can scale. As noted in chapter 1, a strong but flexible culture is the graphene of organizational success. In order to be successful, an ownership mindset needs to permeate the organization and its culture.

Third, remember that as fantastic as an organization's founding vision might be, "what got you here won't get you there" (to paraphrase management coach and author Marshall Goldsmith).[5] In the Community Connections case, the initial approach to service delivery was a quantum leap over what was available elsewhere, but competitors and other models emerged. Only with the addition of a more holistic approach to service delivery (and other changes along the way) could Community Connections survive. As great as those ideas were when first implemented, they would be the 35mm film of photography today—functional but not competitive in the open market.

Sustainability

Most entrepreneurs define sustainability in months or years; some define it in terms of getting to a buy-out of their IPO. Beyond that early-stage, short-term perspective, it is a long way to the centurion status of companies that have been in business for at least a hundred years.[6] Such firms have been the subject of competing business bestsellers, such as *Built to Last: Successful Habits of Visionary Companies* (Jim Collins and Jerry Porras, 1998)[7] and *Creative Destruction: Why Com-*

panies That Are Built to Last Underperform the Market—And How to Successfully Transform Them (Richard Foster and Sarah Kaplan, 2000). Data suggest that destruction is "winning." As noted by various analyses, fewer than one-fifth of Fortune 500 companies in business in 1955 were still running fifty-five to sixty years later.[8] Furthermore, as the BBC News's Kim Gittelson has noted, the average lifespan of S&P 500 companies dropped from sixty-seven years in the 1920s to fifteen years in 2012.[9]

According to the Small Business Administration, small businesses also tend to be short-lived with only one-third surviving ten years or more.[10] However, small to medium size and tight ownership (often family based) are two characteristics of long-lived organizations. Furthermore, small businesses seem to survive for different reasons than large ones. Large firms need to grow to survive; small firms sustain themselves by careful attention to local resources and demand.[11]

In between the star bursts, flameouts, and the centurions are what David Whorton has called "evergreens." They are organizations that "are led by purpose-driven leaders with the grit and resourcefulness to build and scale private, profitable, enduring, and market-leading businesses that make a dent in the universe."[12] Technology company Evernote and its CEO Phil Libin are a good example. He "had this idea of trying to make a hundred-year startup. We decided to take it seriously [which] basically means that there is no short-term."[13]

Although the "evergreen movement" has focused on for-profit entrepreneurial ventures, Community Connections fits squarely in the evergreen category. Research on such firms is scarce, but Whorton characterizes them as having strong doses of seven *P*s:

1. Purpose—passionately driven by a compelling vision and mission
2. Perseverance—the ambition and the resilience to overcome obstacles
3. People First—comprised of a talented team motivated by mission, culture, and compensation, which takes care of the business, customers, suppliers, and community
4. Private—enabling a longer-term view and more operating flexibility
5. Profit—the measuring of success that is the most accurate gauge of customer value

6. Paced Growth—focused on long-term strategy and steady, consistent growth
7. Pragmatic Innovation—continuous improvement based on calculated risks

Although it is a nonprofit and has not always had a long-term strategy, Community Connections has had purpose, perseverance, people, and pragmatism as central, defining attributes since its early days. Being private has facilitated that—both in terms of its separation from government and from the markets.

The fields of strategy, business history, and organizational ecology are all concerned with sustainability and firm longevity. There is no one explanation or answer to the question of why some organizations survive and others don't. There also isn't a consensus about whether longevity is a good thing per se. Being old as an organization isn't necessarily associated with performing well or being "fit"—it might just mean being conservative, small, and staying off competitors' radar.

Recognizing that lack of consensus, some of the most recent research focuses on how plant and animal models can be applied to businesses—given that animal and plant species and human organizations both are inherently complex adaptive systems. Drawing on work in biology, there appear to be three structural principles, which have to do with the design of systems, and three managerial principles, which have to do with the application of intelligence.[14]

As with most things in complex organizations, the principles are somewhat in tension, with managers needing to make complex trade-offs among them. The structural principles include *diversity* (to ensure sufficient diversity of people, ideas, and innovations), *redundancy*, and *modularity* (to buffer against shocks and prevent shocks in one part of the system from crippling the whole). The managerial principles include *prudence* (to reduce risk), *embeddedness* (to foster trust and reciprocity), and *adaptation* (to monitor and adjust to the changing environment). These principles overlap to a considerable degree with others based on analyses of large companies' survival.[15]

As noted earlier, Community Connections's longevity is attributable in part to its ability to adapt to new municipal governments, new competitors, and new business models. Its focus on developing a strong bench is a good example of the diversity and redundancy principles in practice. Prudence and embeddedness are manifest in Community Connections's sound, mission-driven financial management and close ties to its community (enshrined in the organization's name itself). Jim Dewald and Brett Wilson would boil these six principles down to a single one—*a perennially entrepreneurial mindset*.[16] To the extent that they are correct, Community Connections has tried to stay one step ahead in terms of treatment models, holistic approaches to care, and the integration of services throughout its life.

Succession

For organizations to be sustainable across an evergreen (if not centurion) time horizon, they must think about the transition of responsibility from founder/s to others and about succession planning more generally. As noted above, the survival rates are low for small and large firms alike, and family-run businesses (with which Community Connections shares some key characteristics) rarely survive past the third generation of leadership. Research shows that succession planning is one approach to countering these statistics, but there is often resistance to succession planning especially by first-generation family firm leaders and, by extension, founders of other firms.[17] There is also evidence that the benefits of succession planning are greater in the first generation/founder stage of firms' growth than in the second or third generations. At Community Connections, the need to focus on succession planning became painfully clear with the unexpected death of one of its founders.

The advice literature about succession planning/management is extensive. The research regarding succession (especially of CEOs) is extensive too, but the core findings are somewhat limited and often equivocal.[18] The practice of succession planning has generally taken the form of a relay, where the baton gets handed to a specified heir, or a horserace, where multiple heirs compete. In more complicated processes, at organizations like General Electric and Proctor & Gamble, senior executives maintain ranked lists of potential successors and regularly revisit them and their performance.[19] Ultimately, succession planning needs to be the joint responsibility of both the CEO and the board. Without such planning and board involvement in it, organizations risk losing stability, direction, staff focus, retention of current (and potential future) leaders, as well as generating conflict. In contrast, despite resistance to it, succession planning can foster collaboration and *minimize* power struggles. In fact, one study of succession notes that "leaders who are willing to contemplate their retirement and engage in succession planning may be most motivated to grow a firm that is worthy of succession"—an effect referred to as the "shadow of succession."[20]

Although there are many approaches to succession planning, four practices are consistently cited as critical across sectors: (1) leadership development and retention, (2) organizational assessment, (3) clarification of organization direction, and (4) alignment between strategy and goals.[21] Among other tactics that leaders can use is a time-limited leave of absence (e.g., three months) well before their scheduled transition. Such a leave can allow the outgoing leader and current management to test their readiness for the handoff.[22]

SUGGESTED READINGS

There are many good resources regarding succession, but several of the best include Kelin E. Gersick, John A. Davis, Marion McCollom Hampton, and Ivan Lansberg, *Generation to Generation: Life Cycles of the Family Business* (Boston, MA: HBS Press, 1997); Noel Tichy, *Succession: Mastering the Make-or-Break Process of Leadership Transition* (New York: Portfolio, 2014); David Whorton, "The Evergreen Movement: An Emerging Model for Purpose-Driven Entrepreneurs," September 2, 2015, https://www.tugboatinstitute.com/the-evergreen-movement/; and Tim Wolfred, *Building Leaderful Organizations: Succession Planning for Nonprofits* (Annie E. Casey Foundation Executive Transition Monograph Series, 6, 2008).

For a solid summary of the literature on organizational sustainability, see Jim Dewald and W. Brett Wilson, *Achieving Longevity: How Great Firms Prosper through Entrepreneurial Thinking* (Toronto: Rotman-UTP Publishing, 2016); Arie De Geus, *The Living Company: Habits for Survival in a Turbulent Business World* (Boston, MA: HBS Press, 1997); Danny Miller and Isabelle Le Breton-Miller, *Managing for the Long Run: Lessons in Competitive Advantage from Great Family Businesses* (Cambridge, MA: HBS Press, 2005); and Christian Stadler, *Enduring Success: What We Can Learn from the History of Outstanding Corporations* (Redwood City, CA: Stanford University Press, 2011).

For two more extended treatments of how to scale nonprofits and for-profits, respectively, see Kathleen Kelly Janus, *Breakthrough: How the Best Social Startups Scale Up to Change the World* (forthcoming); and Bob Sutton and Huggy Rao, *Scaling Up Excellence: Getting to More Without Settling for Less* (New York: Crown, 2014).

CONCLUSION

Just as every story has an ending, so too does every book. In *Lessons for Nonprofit and Start-Up Leaders: Tales from a Reluctant CEO*, we have tried to tell the story of one organization, Community Connections, and to outline its journey from small start-up to successful social services organization. But we could never have shared all the lessons that were learned over more than three decades, nor could we have articulated all of the issues that any growing organization might face.

Nonprofit organizations like Community Connections are sustained by a shared desire to make the world a better place, whether that is by finding permanent shelter for people living without a stable home, or by working to make the air we breathe cleaner and safer, or by helping endangered animals survive for another generation and beyond. These organizations start with an idea, a mission, but they must learn how to become a business if they are to survive.

The lessons in this book take new CEOs from idea and inspiration, through very pragmatic processes like hiring and interacting with the world outside the organization. And they remind those who start with a sense of their own uniqueness that others have studied and researched and observed organizations like theirs. Remember the first time that you fell in love and you could not imagine that anyone in the whole world had ever felt the way you did—well, just as it wasn't so then, it isn't so now. Others have been there and there is much to learn from their experiences.

The lessons in this book are not only relevant for those in the non-profit world, they apply just as well to inventors, or contractors, or store owners. Everyone has to struggle with who's in charge, whom to hire, and how to plan for the future. For some small companies, the future is a buyout by a bigger company, but for many, there is a desire to grow into an ever more sustainable and successful organization or business, to create something that will survive beyond those who were there at the beginning.

So we take the lessons learned and conclude this book with a fable that just might lead the way into the future.

A FINAL FABLE: WE ARE THE LITTLE BOWLS

In a small village, set between two rivers, the villagers never needed to worry about the supply of water. Each river flowed freely and each supplied the needs of those who lived on its banks. One day, however, a curious event occurred. One of the two rivers began to run dry. What had once been a flowing stream of fresh water was now a hardened riverbed with dry cracks and brown banks that only served to remind villagers of what they had lost.

At first the people on what became known as the dry side of town merely lamented the loss of their beautiful river, but soon they became aware that their supply of water was running dangerously low. No longer were the children seen jumping happily in puddles, nor were the women hanging freshly washed clothing on the lines that hung limp in their yards. The villagers began to worry that there might not be enough water to drink. Without water, there would soon be no life on the dry side of town.

In their desperation, the elders of the dry side turned to their countrymen and women who lived on what become known as the flowing side of town. Since the two groups had once been part of the same big family, they maintained a spirit of cooperation and friendship. Together they thought and thought about what might be done. Finally the leader of the flowing side offered a plan. She would take a very large bowl, one that had been used in clan ceremonies for many years, and dip it into the healthy flowing river that still nourished her side of town. Once the bowl was filled, she would carry it across the whole town—from river-

bank to riverbank—to a large well on the other side. When the well was full, it would supply all the needs of the villagers on the dry side.

With eagerness and a light step, the leader began her long trek from one side of the village to the other. When she was halfway through her journey, she noticed something odd. The large bowl now contained half as much water as when she started. She put the bowl down and looked carefully around, and then she noticed it, a very small hole on one side of the bowl. "Well that solves that," she thought, "I will just walk twice as fast and then I will get to the other side before all the water has leaked out."

But no matter how fast she walked, the water was faster than she was, and each time she arrived at the dry side of town with no water at all left in her bowl.

She put her bowl down and sat by the side of the road and thought and thought. "Perhaps I am just too old and slow to make the trip. If I just found someone younger and faster, she might be able to cross the village with a full bowl of water." She looked at all the young women and girls in the village and found the fastest and strongest to take up the task.

The young woman was confident that she could do what the old leader could not; after all, she was strong and swift. She filled the bowl to the very top and began her run. The faster she went, the more confident she became, but she went so fast that she did not see a rock jutting out from the ground. As she tripped and fell, she was forced to watch as all the cool water splashed over her shiny boots.

"Let me try again," she demanded, but this time she felt herself being pushed back by the force of a strong wind. She fell, crumpled and breathless, to the ground. Everyone knows that it is impossible to fight against the power of the wind. Yet she insisted on trying one more time. But once more she failed to carry the water to the other side of town. The young woman saw the disappointment and fear on the faces of the villagers and then she cast the bowl aside. "This must be a trick," she shouted, "no one can reach the other side with water still in the bowl, no one."

The villagers looked at one another and began to despair that the task was, in fact, just too hard. The young woman was right and the people on the dry side would either have to move or surely die of thirst.

Then the leader heard a small voice, at first so indistinct that it sounded like no more than the wind whistling in the tree branches. But the voice persisted, "Come, dear sister, and I will tell you what you must do. First, you must put the big bowl down. Even though it has the most beautiful colors and a perfect round shape, it was never intended for carrying water all the way across town." The voice that was once soft and muted now spoke with force and authority, commanding the old woman to reach over and pick up a small object resting by her side. "Here, see this little bowl; it is firm and dry and solid. If you fill this bowl with water, you will be able to carry it to the other side without losing a single drop."

Although she was not accustomed to listening to voices that came from outside of her own heart, the old woman had to confess that all of her own ideas had failed. So, with a growing sense of doubt, she filled the little bowl and walked carefully to the other side of town. And to her delight and to the cheers of the villagers, when she arrived her bowl was still filled with water. She poured the water into the big well and before she could even catch her breath, she turned around and began to make the trip again and again and again. By the end of the evening, she had made great progress and the well was almost half full. But the woman was quite exhausted and she thought to herself, "I have done a good job and I have helped to save my brothers and sisters, but I cannot make this trip every day. It is just too hard for me."

Then she heard the voice once again, "You have heard my voice and taken my advice, but you have mistaken my meaning. Of course you are tired. It is much too hard for any one person to satisfy the needs of all the villagers; many will need to help." Just then, the old woman saw a pile of little bowls and she had an idea. She gave one little bowl to each of the waiting villagers, and one by one she filled each of their little bowls with cool water. Together they walked across the town, and with just one trip they filled the entire well to the top.

As they finished pouring the water, they began to shout and dance, "We are the little bowls, we are the little bowls!" And everyone on both sides of town was happy for a very long time.

A PERSONAL NOTE FROM MAXINE

Over the years, as a therapist and a student of individual development, I, like many others, have thought about the stages of life. In the early 1990s I wrote a book, *Down from the Pedestal,* on the stages of a woman's life and chronicled how women moved through at least three distinct phases in their adult lives. In her late teens and twenties, a woman bursts with boundless energy. She has been referred to by some mythologists as a "lady of free and untamed nature." For the young woman, everything seems possible and no challenge seems too big. That was just how Helen and I felt as we embarked on the project that came to be known as Community Connections. If we had realized all that we might face, we might well have turned back, but it was that young woman's naive enthusiasm that propelled us forward.

As a woman reaches the middle of her life, the themes and the challenges change. And so it was with Helen and me. We had birthed a new organization, and now we had to help it grow. I know the analogies with motherhood are obvious, but that is the way it is and it would have been the same if we had been two men. Founding an organization is not the end of the story. You have to tend it, nourish it, and help it sustain itself through hard times. We learned over more than thirty years what we needed to do to make things right and all the ways we could make things go wrong. It is often said that we learn our best lessons from the mistakes we make and that was certainly true for Helen and me.

Helen and I would fantasize that when we retired, we would sit on the porch in two matching rocking chairs and remember all that we had been through. We would have laughed, and sighed, and shaken our heads. Helen never made it to that porch, but rocking and remembering and putting things in perspective are the challenges that men and women face as they look back on their accomplishments. As Community Connections moved into its fourth decade, the time came to look back, not to stop looking forward, but to look back and understand what had been created and what could be left behind.

I could have told this story myself, as somewhat of a personal memoir, but Michael has helped to make it so much more. My story is not solely mine. It exists in the context of other similar stories. Helen and I painted our picture, but Michael reminds us that there are only so many colors on the palette.

WHERE IS COMMUNITY CONNECTIONS NOW?

As it enters its fourth decade, some things about Community Connections are the same as they were when it opened its doors in 1984. It still provides behavioral and mental health services, and still provides housing for the homeless and recovery programs for people with addictions. Community Connections continues to do research and test out new models of care, and it addresses the mental health needs of children and families. But it has not remained static; it has added new programs: primary health care and pharmacy services; testing and counseling for people with HIV; and supported employment for transitioning youth, people leaving the criminal justice system, and those who have never been employed.

Perhaps the most obvious change is that Community Connections is bigger. It serves one hundred times more people, employs over a hundred times more staff, and occupies much more space. It has spread to all parts of the District of Columbia, including, in 2016, to the poorest ward, "the ward across the bridge."

However, something far more important has changed, and that is how the organization sees itself when it looks in the mirror. The name "Community Connections" embodied the idea that helping people connect to existing communities was its primary mission, and that is still true. But there is a new realization that Community Connections has become its own community, shifting wherever possible to referring to the people who receive services as "people," rather than as "patients" or "clients." Language has a powerful impact and words that emphasize similarity rather than difference say loud and clear that we are all part of the same community. As the song says, "We Are the World."

Community Connections has been a leader in including peers (people who have been through similar experiences themselves) in the work of recovery. For years, the addictions movement has looked within its own ranks for healing. Community Connections now employs peers in every aspect of its programming. Families help families; abused women reach out to one another; people in crisis learn from others who have gone through the same struggles. Health care is not only delivered by professionals but is also supported by peers who work toward building a community of healthy people. In 1972, songwriter Bill Withers wrote the classic "Lean on Me." We will all need someone to lean on at some time in our lives, so we should reach out and offer a hand to those who are in need now, and peers do that best.

Just as Community Connections is a community, it also belongs to a community. Community *is* connection. Programs to reach out to local neighbors and businesses, to partner with developers and community organizers, to reach out to the courts and the schools and the local police department all speak to the recognition that we only thrive when we realize that we are all in this together. And as Community Connections has reached out to neighbors and local businesses, they have reached back, bringing opportunity for collaboration and acceptance with them. Even campaign and corporate slogans in 2016 argued for connection. The Democrats appealed for us to be stronger together, and Apple celebrated Christmas with a television ad showing people in a quaint town welcoming a Frankenstein character with an appeal to open our hearts to everyone. Even the energy giant Koch Industries initiated a campaign to "end the divide" that separated people.

A growing commitment to community has opened the organization to understanding the role that social justice plays in furthering the core business. Community Connections recognizes that poverty and discrimination and stigma have all made recovery from psychiatric and behavioral problems more difficult. And it now raises money for school supplies and school uniforms for disadvantaged children, obtains government subsidies for housing homeless people, provides training opportunities and jobs for peers who want to move into the mental health field, supports mothers who receive welfare benefits, and provides food for the holidays to those in need. The organization works within the criminal justice system to provide behavioral health services as an alternative to incarceration, especially for young offenders.

Community Connections has moved beyond solely providing behavioral and mental health services. When you drop a pebble in the lake, the ripples spread out in concentric circles. Community Connections's world has spread beyond the small circle of the individual to the larger ring of the family and then to the limits of its own boundaries, until finally it has joined the ripple of the entire community. It has grown in size, but also in vision.

NOTES

INTRODUCTION

1. Patrick Lencioni, *Five Temptations of a CEO* (San Francisco: Jossey-Bass, 2008).

I. EVERY ORGANIZATION HAS A CULTURE OF ITS OWN

1. *Wikipedia*, s.v. "St. Elizabeths Hospital," accessed December 27, 2016, https://en.wikipedia.org/wiki/St._Elizabeths_Hospital.

2. Mike DeBonis, "D.C. Near Settlement in Mental Health Case," *Washington Post*, September 20, 2011, accessed December 25, 2016, https://www.washingtonpost.com/local/dc-politics/dc-near-settlement-in-mental-health-case/2011/09/12/gIQA9nq4NK_story.html?utm_term=.1809e9498011.

3. Maxine Harris and Helen Bergman, eds., *Case Management for Mentally Ill Patients* (Boca Raton, FL: CRC Press, 1993).

4. Maxine Harris, *Sisters of the Shadow* (Norman: University of Oklahoma Press, 1991).

5. This section draws heavily on the work of Ed Schein, one of the foremost scholars of organizational culture. Kim Cameron and Robert Quinn's Competing Values Framework is the other, most widely used model of culture. Note also that this chapter focuses on organizational culture, not national culture, about which there is a vast but mostly separate literature.

6. On such relationships with culture, see for example, Jesper B. Sorensen, "The Strength of Corporate Culture and the Reliability of Firm Performance," *Administrative Science Quarterly* 47 (2002): 70–91; and Anthony S. Boyce et

al., "Which Comes First, Organizational Culture or Performance? A Longitudinal Study of Causal Priority with Automobile Dealerships," *Journal of Organizational Behavior* 36, no. 3 (2015): 339–59.

7. Although Drucker certainly would have agreed in spirit, a close search of his writings suggests that he didn't actually say this, despite how many attribute it to him.

8. Robert H. Waterman, Thomas J. Peters, and Julien R. Phillips, "Structure Is Not Organization," *Business Horizons* 23, no. 3 (1980): 14–26; David A. Nadler and Michael L. Tushman, "A Model for Diagnosing Organizational Behavior," *Organizational Dynamics* 9, no. 2 (1980): 35–51; W. Warner Burke and George H. Litwin, "A Causal Model of Organizational Performance and Change," *Journal of Management* 18, no. 3 (1992): 523–45.

9. Reid Hastings, Netflix, "Reference Guide on Culture," 2009, slide 8, accessed February 13, 2017, https://www.slideshare.net/reed2001/culture-2009/8-The_real_company_values_as.

10. Hastings, "Reference Guide on Culture," slide 127, https://www.slideshare.net/reed2001/culture-2009/127-Need_a_culture_that_avoids.

11. Jennifer A. Chatman et al., "Parsing Organizational Culture: How the Norm for Adaptability Influences the Relationship between Culture Consensus and Financial Performance in High-Technology Firms," *Journal of Organizational Behavior* 35, no. 6 (2014): 785–808.

12. For a recent discussion of this tendency to blame or start with culture, see Jay Lorsch and Emily McTague, "Culture Is Not the Culprit," *Harvard Business Review*, April 2016, 2–11.

2. HOW TO MAKE AN IDEA COME ALIVE

1. John F. Kennedy, Address to Congress on Urgent National Needs, May 25, 1961, accessed December 24, 2016, https://www.jfklibrary.org/JFK/JFK-Legacy/NASA-Moon-Landing.aspx.

2. Goodreads.com, s.v. "Albert Einstein," accessed December 24, 2016, http://www.goodreads.com/quotes/139925-imagination-is-the-highest-form-of-research.

3. BrainyQuote.com, s.v. "Saul Bellow," accessed December 24, 2016, https://www.brainyquote.com/quotes/quotes/s/saulbellow136446.html.

4. Goodreads.com, s.v. "Wendell Berry," accessed December 24, 2016, http://www.goodreads.com/quotes/24729-there-are-it-seems-two-muses-the-muse-of-inspiration.

5. "Mark Zuckerberg's Letter to Investors," *Wired*, February 1, 2012, https://www.wired.com/2012/02/zuck-letter/, accessed September 24, 2016.

6. Jim Collins and Morton Hansen, *Great by Choice* (New York: Harper Business, 2011).

7. BrainyQuote.com, s.v. "Thomas Jefferson," accessed December 24, 2016, https://www.brainyquote.com/quotes/quotes/t/thomasjeff120901.html.

8. BrainyQuote.com, s.v. "Thomas A. Edison," accessed December 24, 2016, https://www.brainyquote.com/quotes/quotes/t/thomasaed109928.html.

9. Jeanne Liedtka's work (see the following note) has begun to push for more explicit and scientific understanding of design thinking's effects.

10. See especially Jeanne Liedtka, Andrew King, and Kevin Bennett, *Solving Problems with Design Thinking: Ten Stories of What Works* (New York: Columbia Business School Press, 2013) and Jeanne Liedtka, "Perspective: Linking Design Thinking with Innovation Outcomes through Cognitive Bias Reduction," *Journal of Product Innovation Management* 32 (2015): 925–38.

3. POWER, AUTHORITY, AND RESPONSIBILITY

1. *Steve Jobs*, directed by Danny Boyle, Universal Pictures, 2015.

2. Harry S. Truman Library and Museum, "The Buck Stops Here" desk sign, accessed December 24, 2016, https://www.trumanlibrary.org/buckstop.htm.

3. William Shakespeare, *King Henry IV, Part 2* (New York: Simon and Schuster, 2006), act 3, scene 1.

4. William Shakespeare, *Julius Caesar* (New York: Simon and Shuster, 2004), act 1, scene 2.

5. Carol Gilligan, *In a Different Voice* (Cambridge, MA: Harvard University Press, 1982).

6. BrainyQuote.com, s.v. "Abraham Lincoln," accessed December 24, 2016, https://www.brainyquote.com/quotes/quotes/a/abrahamlin101343.html.

7. BrainyQuote.com, s.v. "Margaret Thatcher," accessed December 24, 2016, https://www.brainyquote.com/quotes/quotes/m/margaretth109592.html.

8. *Wikipedia*, s.v. "Rumpole of the Bailey," accessed December 24, 2016, https://en.wikipedia.org/wiki/Rumpole_of_the_Bailey.

9. *Wikipedia*, s.v. "*She: A History of Adventure*," accessed December 24, 2016, https://en.wikipedia.org/wiki/She:_A_History_of_Adventure.

10. Brainyquote.com, s.v. "Lord Acton," accessed December 24, 2016, https://www.brainyquote.com/search_results?q=lord%20acton.

11. Jeffrey Pfeffer, *Power: Why Some People Have It—And Others Don't* (New York: HarperCollins, 2010).

12. Noam Wasserman, *The Founder's Dilemmas: Anticipating and Avoiding the Pitfalls That Can Sink a Startup* (Princeton, NJ: Princeton University Press, 2012).

13. K. M. Eisenhardt and L. J. Bourgeois, "Politics of Strategic Decision Making in High-Velocity Environments: Toward a Midrange Theory," *Academy of Management Journal* 31 (1988): 737–70; and J. Haleblian and S. Finkelstein, "Top Management Team Size, CEO Dominance, and Firm Performance: The Moderating Roles of Environmental Turbulence and Discretion," *Academy of Management Journal* 36 (1999): 844–63.

14. S. A. Dennis, D. Ramsey, and C. Turner, "Dual or Duel: Co-CEOs and Firm Performance," *Journal of Business and Economic Studies* 15 (2009):1–25.

15. R. Krause, R. Priem, and L. Love, "Who's In Charge Here? Co-CEOs, Power Gaps, and Firm Performance," *Strategic Management Journal* 36 (2015): 2099–110.

16. Matteo P. Arena, Stephen P. Ferris, and Emre Unlu, "It Takes Two: The Incidence and Effectiveness of Co-CEOs," *Financial Review* 46 (2011): 385–412.

4. HIRING

1. For example, see M. Bidwell and J. R. Keller, "Within or Without? How Firms Combine Internal and External Labor Markets to Fill Jobs," *Academy of Management Journal* 57 (2014): 1035–55; and M. Bidwell and E. Mollick, "Shifts and Ladders: Comparing the Role of Internal and External Mobility in Managerial Careers," *Organization Science* 26 (2015): 1629–45.

2. Rui Wang, *The Chinese Imperial Examination System: An Annotated Bibliography* (Toronto: Scarecrow Press, 2013).

3. S. L. Rynes, et al., "The Very Separate Worlds of Academic and Practitioner Periodicals in Human Resource Management: Implications for Evidence-Based Management," *Academy of Management Journal* 50 (2007): 987–1008.

4. T. Minton-Eversole, "Quality Measurement: Key to Best-in-Class Talent Acquisition," *HR Magazine* (2009): 64–65.

5. J. A. Breaugh, *Recruiting and Attracting Talent* (Alexandria, VA: SHRM, 2016).

6. A. M. Ryan and N. T. Tippins, "Not Much More Than Platitudes: A Critical Look at the Utility of Applicant Reactions Research," *Human Resources Management Review* 18 (2008): 119–32.

7. A. E. Colbert, S. L. Rynes, and K. G. Brown, "Understanding Managers' Agreement with Human Resource Research Findings," *Journal of Applied Behavioral Science* 41 (2007): 304–25.

8. "Shhhh! Companies Would Benefit from Helping Introverts to Thrive," *The Economist*, September 9, 2016, 59.

9. S. L. Rynes, K. G. Brown, and A. E. Colbert, "Seven Common Misconceptions about Human Resource Practices: Research Findings versus Practitioner Beliefs," *Academy of Management Executive* 16 (2002): 92–103.

10. A. M. Ryan and N. T. Tippins, "Attracting and Selecting: What Psychological Research Tells Us," *Human Resource Management* 43 (2004): 305–18.

11. Ryan and Tippins, "Attracting and Selecting."

12. Ryan and Tippins, "Attracting and Selecting."

13. Adapted and abridged from Ryan and Tippins, "Attracting and Selecting."

5. BARRIERS TO SOLVING PROBLEMS

1. BrainyQuote.com, s.v. "Edmund Wilson," https://www.brainyquote.com/quotes/quotes/e/edmundwils110105.html, accessed December 25, 2016.

2. Goodreads.com, s.v. "Abraham Lincoln," http://www.goodreads.com/quotes/67318-we-can-complain-because-rose-bushes-have-thorns-or-rejoice, accessed December 25, 2016.

3. Poemhunter.com, s.v. "Oscar Wilde," http://www.poemhunter.com/quotations/famous.asp?people=Oscar%20Wilde&p=21, accessed December 25, 2016.

4. N. Dries, T. Vantilborgh, and R. Pepermans, "The Role of Learning Agility and Career Variety in the Identification and Development of High Potential Employees," *Personnel Review*, 41 (2012): 340–58.

6. ENGAGING THE OUTSIDE WORLD

1. Dixon v. Weinberger, District of Columbia District Court, Case No. 74-285 docket://gov.uscourts.dcd.74-285, accessed December 25, 2016, http://www.plainsite.org/dockets/1zjkb13yx/district-of-columbia-district-court/dixon-v-weinberger/.

2. Although this expression is often attributed to Phineas T. Barnum, this has not been substantiated.

3. Brad Tuttle, "5 Awesome Old-School TV Ads for Financial Service Companies," *Money*, accessed December 25, 2016, http://time.com/money/3751765/ef-hutton-old-financial-service-ads/.

4. Maxine Harris, *Trauma Recovery and Empowerment* (New York: The Free Press, 1998).

5. Jim Collins and Morton T. Hansen, *Great by Choice* (New York: Harper Business, 2011).

6. Substance Abuse and Mental Health Services Administration, "About Recovery Month," accessed December 25, 2016, https://recoverymonth.gov/about.

7. AZ Quotes, s.v. "J. Vernon Magee," accessed December 25, 2016, http://www.azquotes.com/quote/1394172.

8. BrainyQuote.com, s.v. "Benjamin Franklin," accessed December 25, 2016, https://www.brainyquote.com/quotes/quotes/b/benjaminfr151622.html.

9. Mark Smith, interview by Travis Good, *The Healthcare Innovators Podcast*, Catalyze, April 26, 2016, accessed December 26, 2016, https://catalyze.io/innovation/mark-smith-md.

10. John Donne, "No Man Is an Island," accessed December 25, 2016, http://www.poemhunter.com/poem/no-man-is-an-island/.

11. Barry M. Staw, Lloyd Sandelands, and Jane E. Dutton, "Threat Rigidity Effects in Organizational Behavior: A Multilevel Analysis," *Administrative Science Quarterly* 26, no. 4 (1981): 501–24.

12. Deborah Ancona, Henrik Bresman, and Katrin Käufer, "The Comparative Advantage of X-Teams," *MIT Sloan Management Review* 43, no. 3 (2002): 33.

13. Daniel Kahneman, *Thinking, Fast and Slow* (New York: Doubleday, 2011).

14. C. J. Gersick and J. R. Hackman, "Habitual Routines in Task-Performing Groups," *Organizational Behavior and Human Decision Processes* 47 (1990): 65–97.

7. THE IMPORTANCE OF SELF AND ORGANIZATIONAL AWARENESS

1. William Shakespeare, *Hamlet,* Folger Library Shakespeare (New York: Simon & Schuster, 1992), act 2, scene 7.

2. William Shakespeare, *As You Like It,* Folger Library Shakespeare (New York: Simon & Schuster, 2004), act 1, scene 3.

3. Plato, *Apology*, accessed December 26, 2016, https://en.wikipedia.org/wiki/The_unexamined_life_is_not_worth_living.

4. BrainyQuote.com, s.v. "Bob Seger," accessed December 26, 2016, https://www.brainyquote.com/quotes/quotes/b/bobseger106054.html.

5. D. Dunning, C. Heath, and J. M. Suls, "Flawed Self-Assessment Implications for Health, Education, and the Workplace," *Psychological Science in the Public Interest* 5 (2004): 69–106.

6. Their work actually refers to two effects: (1) The tendency for low-ability people to overestimate their ability (e.g., bad drivers think they're good drivers), and (2) The tendency for high-ability people to underestimate their relative competence and assume that tasks that are easy for them are also easy for others.

7. J. Kruger and D. Dunning, "Unskilled and Unaware of It: How Difficulties in Recognizing One's Own Incompetence Lead to Inflated Self-Assessments," *Journal of Personality and Social Psychology* 77 (1999): 1121–34.

8. D. A. Davis, P. E. Mazmanian, M. Fordis, R. Van Harrison, K. E. Thorpe, and L. Perrier, "Accuracy of Physician Self-Assessment Compared with Observed Measures of Competence: A Systematic Review," *JAMA* 296, no. 9 (2006):1094–102; K. P. Cross, "Not Can, But Will College Teaching Be Improved?" *New Directions for Higher Education* 17 (1977): 1–15;, N. Falchikov and D. Boud, "Student Self-Assessment in Higher Education: A Meta-Analysis," *Review of Educational Research* 594 (1989): 395–430.

9. P. A. Mabe and S. G. West, "Validity of Self-Evaluation of Ability: A Review and Meta-Analysis," *Journal of Applied Psychology* 67 (1982): 280–96.

10. D. Dunning, C. Heath, and J. M. Suls, "Flawed Self-Assessment Implications for Health, Education, and the Workplace," *Psychological Science in the Public Interest* 5 (2004): 69–106.

11. D. A. Risucci, A. J. Tortolani, and R. J. Ward, "Ratings of Surgical Residents by Self, Supervisors and Peers," *Surgery, Gynecology & Obstetrics* 169 (1989): 519–26.

12. B. M. Bass and F. J. Yammarino, "Congruence of Self and Others' Leadership Ratings of Naval Officers for Understanding Successful Performance," *Applied Psychology* 40 (1991): 437–54.

13. N. Epley and D. Dunning, "The Mixed Blessings of Self-Knowledge in Behavioral Prediction," *Personality and Social Psychology Bulletin* 32, no. 5 (2006): 641–55. http://journals.sagepub.com/doi/abs/10.1177/0146167205284007?url_ver=Z39.88-2003&rfr_id=ori:rid:crossref.org&rfr_dat=cr_pub%3dpubmed.

14. D. Dunning, *Self-insight: Roadblocks and Detours on the Path to Knowing Thyself* (New York: Psychology Press, 2012).

15. Dunning, Heath, and Suls, "Flawed Self-Assessment."

16. R. Amler, D. Moriarty, and E. Hutchins, *Healthier People* (Decatur, GA: Carter Center of Emory University Health Risk Appraisal Program, 1989).

8. PREPARING FOR THE FUTURE

1. National Academies Collection, "Coordinating Care for Better Mental, Substance-Use, and General Health," in *Improving the Quality of Health Care for Mental and Substance Abuse Conditions* (Washington, DC: National Academies Press) accessed December 26, 2016, https://www.ncbi.nlm.nih.gov/books/NBK19833/.

2. "Sister Irene Kraus Remembered for Vision, Leadership 08/25/98," *Florida Times Union*, August 25, 1998, accessed December 25, 2016, http://jacksonville.com/tu-online/stories/082598/met_2a1Siste.html.

3. Tanya Somanader, "In Memory of Beau Biden: 'Quite Simply, the Finest Man Any of Us Have Ever Known,'" The White House of President Barack Obama blog, accessed January 26, 2017, https://obamawhitehouse.archives.gov/blog/2015/05/30/memory-beau-biden-quite-simply-finest-man-any-us-have-ever-known.

4. Bob Sutton and Huggy Rao, *Scaling Up Excellence: Getting to More Without Settling for Less* (New York: Crown, 2014).

5. Marshall Goldsmith and Mark Reiter, *What Got You Here Won't Get You There* (New York: Hachette Book Group, 2007).

6. Note that longevity varies widely by country. In the United States, a century has generally been considered an extremely long run for a company, but in Japan and Europe, older companies are more common. In Japan, France, and the UK, they have their own societies: Shinise (100+ years), Les Henokiens (200+ years), and the Tercentenarians (300+ years).

7. Other general audience books in this tradition include A. de Geus, *The Living Company: Habits for Survival in a Turbulent Business World* (Boston, MA: Harvard Business Review Press, 1997); D. Miller and I. Le Breton-Miller, *Managing for the Long Run: Lessons in Competitive Advantage from Great Family Businesses* (Cambridge, MA: Harvard Business Review Press, 2005); and C. Stadler, *Enduring Success: What We Can Learn from the History of Outstanding Corporations* (Redwood City, CA: Stanford University Press, 2011).

8. M. J. Perry, "Fortune 500 firms in 1955 vs. 2014," AEIdeas, August 18, 2014, accessed October 10, 2016, https://www.aei.org/publication/fortune-500-firms-in-1955-vs-2014–89-are-gone-and-were-all-better-off-because-of-that-dynamic-creative-destruction/.

9. Kim Gittelson, "Can a Company Live Forever?" BBC News, January 19, 2012, accessed February 13, 2017, http://www.bbc.com/news/business-16611040.

10. Small Business Administration, "FAQs about Small Businesses," September 2012, https://www.sba.gov/sites/default/files/FAQ_Sept_2012.pdf.

11. M. R. Napolitano, V. Marino, A. Riviezzo, and A. Garofano, "Moving Forward or Running to Stand Still? The Relationship between Family Firms' Strategic Posture and Longevity." Paper presented at the AIDEA Bicentenary Conference, Lecce, 2013.

12. David Whorton, "The Evergreen Movement: An Emerging Model for Purpose-Driven Entrepreneurs," September 2, 2015, https://www.tugboatinstitute.com/the-evergreen-movement/.

13. P. Libin, "Evernote's Quest to Become a 100-Year-Old Startup," *Fast-Company*, June 13, 2013, https://www.fastcompany.com/3012870/dialed/evernotes-quest-to-become-a-100-year-old-startup.

14. M. Reeves, S. Levin, and D. Ueda, 2016. "The Biology of Corporate Survival," *Harvard Business Review* (January-February 2016): 47–55.

15. C. Stadler, "The Four Principles of Enduring Success," *Harvard Business Review* 85 (2007): 62–72; and C. Stadler *Enduring Success: What We Can Learn from the History of Outstanding Corporations* (Redwood City, CA: Stanford University Press, 2011). Stadler focuses on four principles—diversity (in suppliers and customers); a willingness to remember, discuss, and learn from mistakes; a tendency to exploit before exploring; and a general conservatism regarding change.

16. Jim Dewald and W. Brett Wilson, *Achieving Longevity: How Great Firms Prosper through Entrepreneurial Thinking* (Toronto: Rotman-UTP Publishing, 2016).

17. K. A. Eddleston, F. W. Kellermanns, S. W. Floyd, V. L. Crittenden, and W. F. Crittenden, "Planning for Growth: Life Stage Differences in Family Firms," *Entrepreneurship Theory and Practice* 37 (2013): 1177–1202.

18. K. Froelich, G. McKee, and R. Rathge, "Succession Planning in Non-profit Organizations," *Nonprofit Management and Leadership* 22 (2011): 3–20.

19. A. G. Lafley and N. M. Tichy, "The Art and Science of Finding the Right CEO," *Harvard Business Review*, October 2011, 3–10.

20. Eddleston et al., "Planning for Growth."

21. S. Gothard and M. J. Austin, "Leadership Succession Planning: Implications for Non-profit Human Service Organizations," *Administration in Social Work* 37, no. 3 (2013): 272–85.

22. Tim Wolfred, *Building Leaderful Organizations: Succession Planning for Nonprofits* (Annie E. Casey Foundation Executive Transition Monograph Series, 6, 2008).

INDEX

MIT Media Lab, 35
modularity, 153
Mozart, Wolfgang Amadeus, 24

Netflix, 17–18
Newton, Isaac, 25

Oracle, 59
office space, 142
organizational awareness, 127–128
organizational chart, 46, 64–65, 147
organizational culture, 14–15, 151;
    artifacts, 14–15; assumptions
    underlying, 14; levers of change, 2–3,
    strength, attributes of, 16–17; values
    exposed, 14

peer-delivered services, 145, 162
Pfeffer, Jeffrey, 56
physical abuse. *See* trauma and abuse
Porras, Jerry, 151
Power,: abuse of, 52; accountability and,
    54, 57; acquisition of, 45; authority
    versus, 44, 53, 57; denial of, 48–49;
    definition,; difficulty using, 46–47;
    generational passage, 45, 49; giving
    away, 49–51; in social service agencies,
    48; influence and, 56–57; leadership
    and, 56; responsibility and, 54, 57;
    struggles involving, 154; women and,
    51
problem-solving: framing, 88–89,
    100–101; perspective and, 86, 89–92
Proctor & Gamble, 154
prudence, 153

Rao, Huggy, 151
redundancy, 153
RIM, 59
Rumpole of the Bailey, 55

Salieri, Antonio, 24
Sandelands, Lloyd, 117
SAP, 35
Seger, Bob, 131
seven *Ps*. *See* evergreen companies
sexual abuse. *See* trauma and abuse

scalability, 140–142, 150–153
self-assessment. *See* self-awareness
self-awareness, 124, 134; accuracy of,
    132–134; enhancing quality. *See*
    feedback
Shakespeare, William, 121, 124
She Who Must Be Obeyed, 55
Sisters of the Shadow, 9
Smith Barney, 108
social justice, 163
St. Elizabeths Hospital, 3–4, 4, 7, 106;
    history of, 3; relationship to the outside
    world, 4
Staw, Barry, 117
succession planning, 50, 147–149,
    154–155; drop dead plan, 148
sustainability, 151–154
Sutton, Bob, 151

TCAP, 146
teenage pregnancy, 141
thinking it through. *See* ideation
Toyota, 36
training staff, 145
trauma and abuse, 12, 28, 145; groups, 29
Trauma Recovery and Empowerment
    model, 110–111
treatment models, 154
Truman, Harry, 44
Twain, Mark, 114

unemployment, 32, 140

Volkswagon, 58

Whole Foods, 59
Whorton, David, 152
Wilde, Oscar, 86
Wilson, Brett, 154
Wilson, Edmund, 86
Winterkorn, Martin, 58
Withers, Bill, 162
Wozniak, Steve, 44

Zappos, 17
Zuckerberg, Mark, 26

ABOUT THE AUTHORS

Maxine Harris, PhD, is the cofounder and current CEO of Community Connections, a large behavioral health care organization located in the nation's capital. She has been operating Community Connections (in conjunction with her now-deceased partner Helen Bergman) for more than thirty years.

Dr. Harris is a national expert in clinical practices for treating persons with serious mental illness, substance addiction, homelessness, trauma, domestic violence, and early traumatic loss. She has authored or edited nine books and ten training manuals on these topics and has served as keynote speaker at several national conferences. Her most successful book, *The Loss That Is Forever: The Lifelong Impact of the Early Death of a Mother or Father,* was published in 1995 and is still in print after more than twenty years.

Dr. Harris is the recipient of the first HOPE award, granted by the federal Center for Mental Health Services for her "pioneering work and innovation in the field of trauma-informed care." She has also served as the principal investigator on federal grants studying homelessness, trauma, addiction, HIV infection, and residential services.

Michael B. O'Leary, PhD, is professor at Georgetown's McDonough School of Business and was previously a faculty member at Boston College, a policy analyst for Pelavin Associates, and a management consultant at C&L. In addition to undergraduate, master's, and doctoral students, he has taught executive programs for a wide variety of domestic and international organizations. He is the co-designer and lead academic advisor of the Presidential Leadership Scholars Program, which is sponsored jointly by the foundations and libraries of Presidents Bush (41 and 43), Clinton, and Johnson.

Prior to his academic career, he worked on large-scale reorganizations, technology implementations, and process redesigns. His clients included universities, major medical centers, large nonprofits, and government agencies.

His research focuses on high-performing teams (especially virtual ones), multitasking, multiteaming, and teams facing resource constraints.